RECORDED VERSIONS
GUITAR

ISBN 0-634-03999-7

HAL•LEONARD®
CORPORATION

7777 W. BLUEMOUND RD. P.O. BOX 13819 MILWAUKEE, WI 53213

Visit Hal Leonard Online at
www.halleonard.com

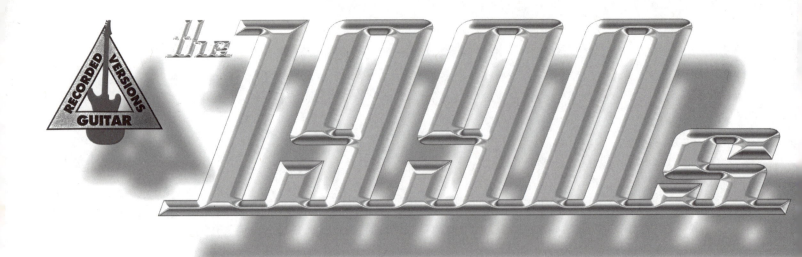

CONTENTS

All I Wanna Do

Words and Music by Kevin Gilbert, David Baerwald, Sheryl Crow, Wyn Cooper and Bill Bottrell

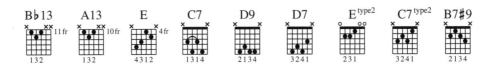

Gtr. 1 tuning:
(low to high) E–A–D–G#–B–E

Intro

Moderately ♩ = 124

* Pedal steel arr. for gtr. Wear slide on pinky throughout.

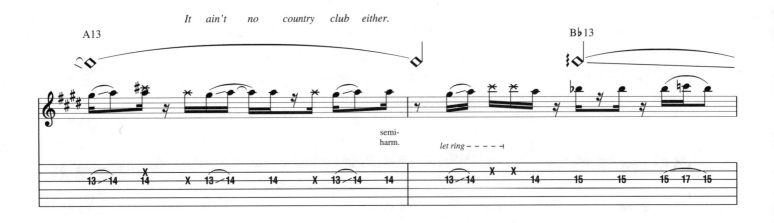

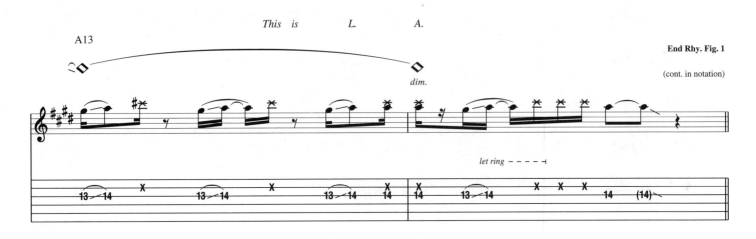

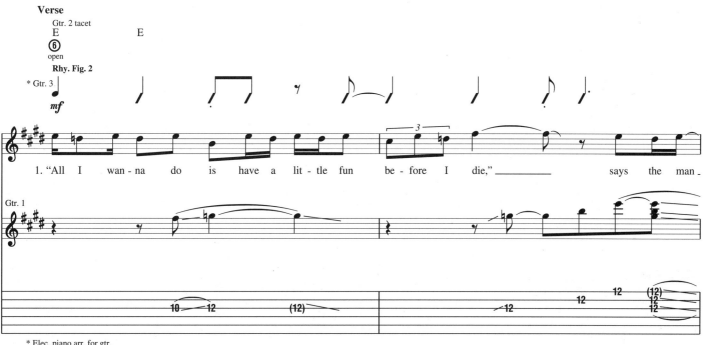

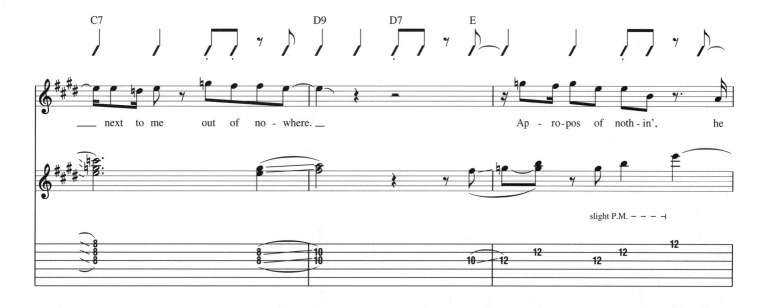

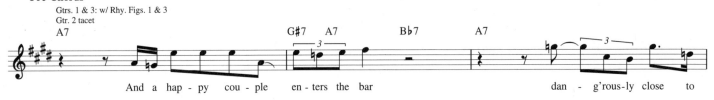

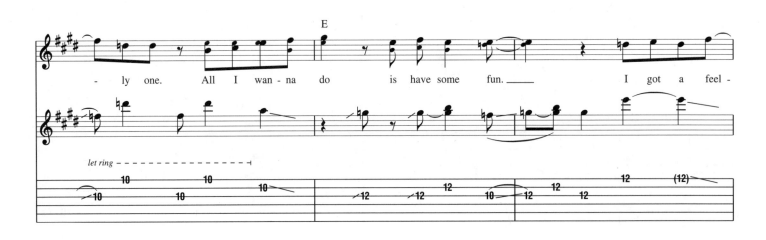

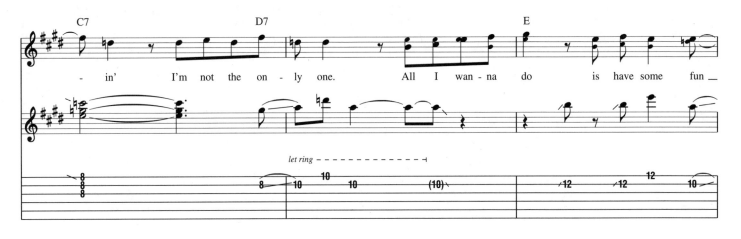

car wash, too. _____ The match - es and the Buds and

Gtrs. 1 & 3: w/ Rhy. Figs. 1 & 3 (last 2 meas.)

the clean ___ and dirt - y cars, the sun and the moon. But all I wan - na

Chorus

Gtr. 4: w/ Rhy. Fig. 4 (4 1/2 times)

do is have some fun. ___ I got a feel - in' I'm not the on -

Gtr. 1

w/ slide

let ring - - - - - - - - - - - - - - - - -

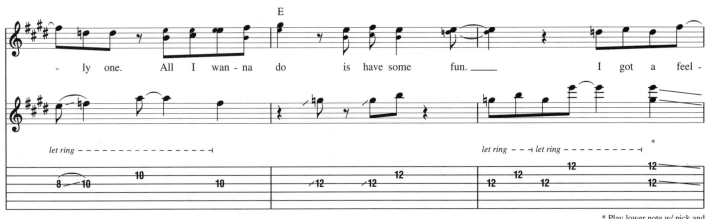

- ly one. All I wan - na do is have some fun. ___ I got a feel -

let ring - - - - - - - - - - - - - -   let ring - - - - let ring - - - - - - - - -   *

* Play lower note w/ pick and
higher note w/ R.H. finger.

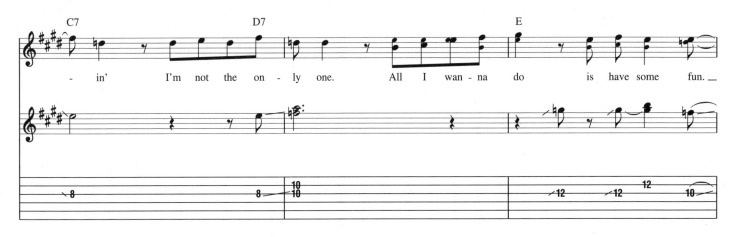

- in' I'm not the on - ly one. All I wan - na do is have some fun.

Gtr. 4: w/ Rhy. Fig. 4 (2 1/2 times)

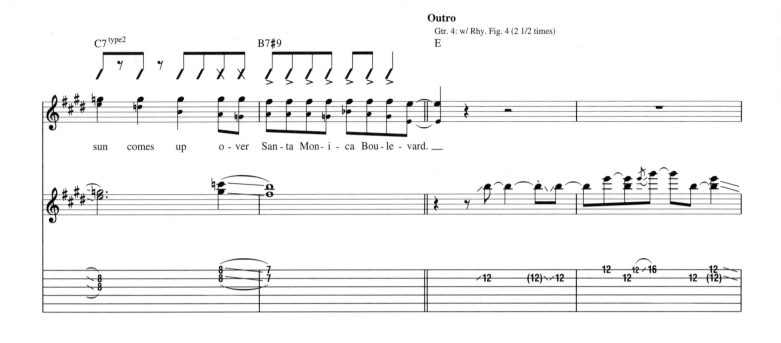

sun comes up o - ver San - ta Mon - i - ca Bou - le - vard.

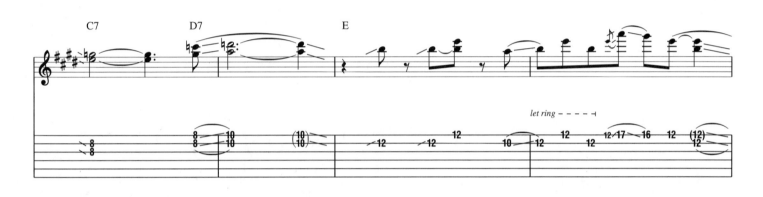

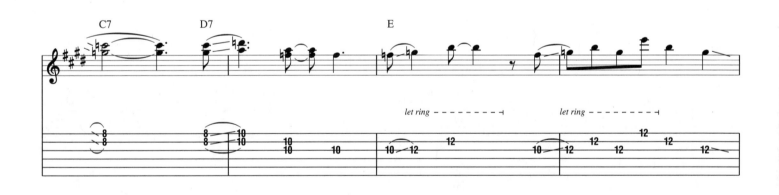

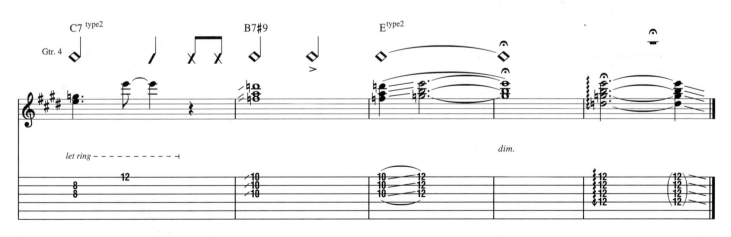

Are You Gonna Go My Way

Words by Lenny Kravitz

Music by Lenny Kravitz and Craig Ross

*Chord symbols reflect implied harmony.

So that's why_____ you got to try.
So tell me why_____ we got to die

*T = Thumb on 6th str.

2nd time, Gtr. 2: w/Fill 1

You got to breathe and have some fun.
and kill each oth-er one by one.

Fill 1

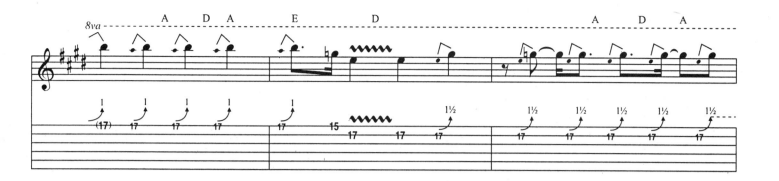

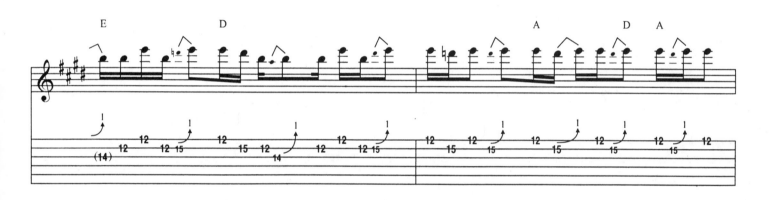

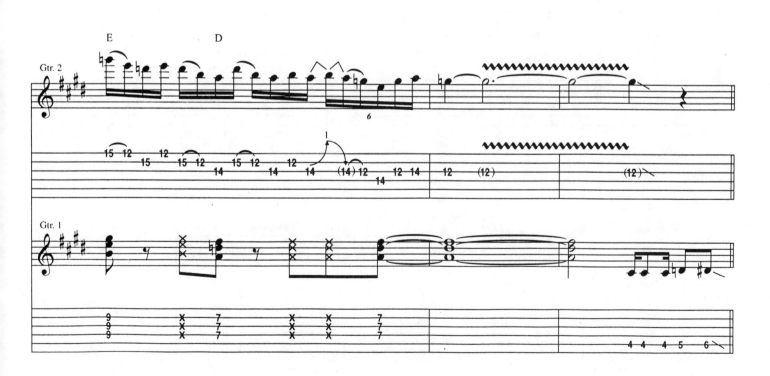

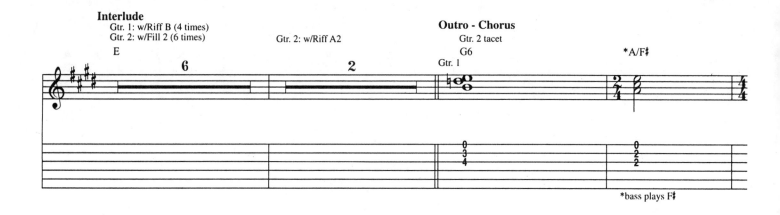

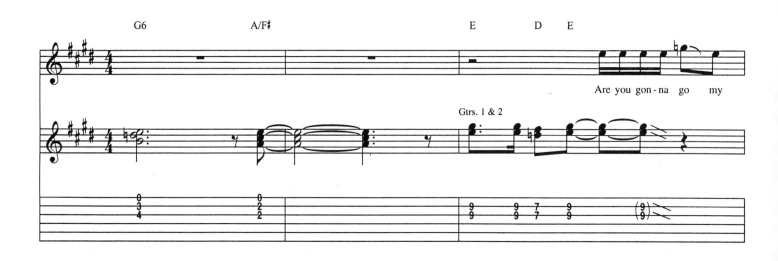

Barely Breathing

Words and Music by Duncan Sheik

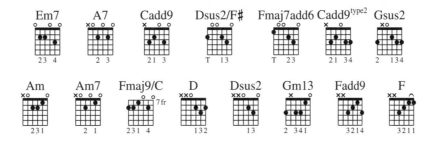

Intro
Moderately ♩ = 94

*Two gtrs. arr. for one.

22

To Coda ⊕

Chorus

23

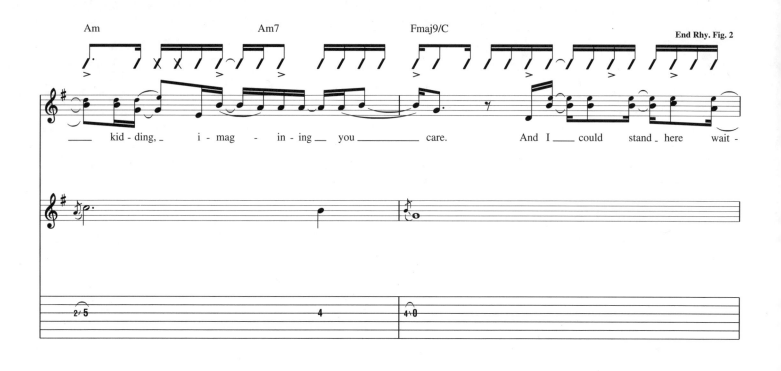

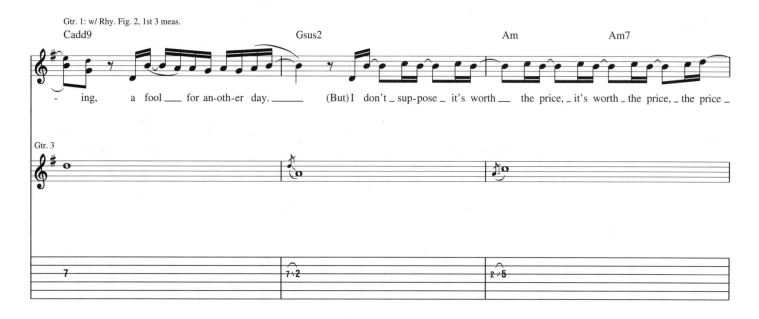

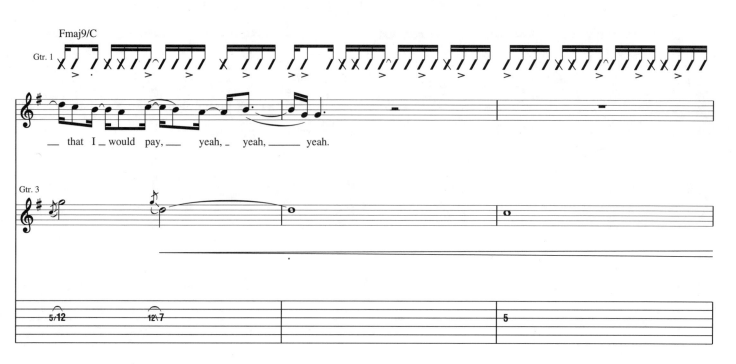

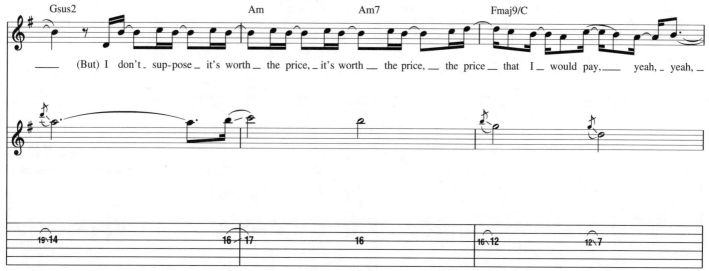

Cadd9　　　　　　　　　　　Gsus2　　　　　　　　　Am　　Am7

_____ yeah.　　　But I'm think-ing　it　o　-　ver　　an　-　y　-　way. _____

*Gtr. 4 (elec.)

Gtr. 3
divisi

**

*w/E-bow & dist.
**Gtr. 4 to right of slashes.

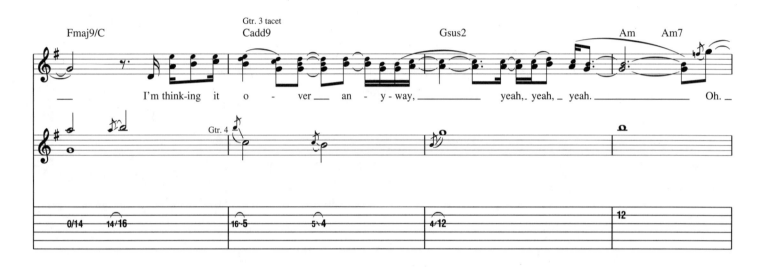

Fmaj9/C　　　　　　　　Gtr. 3 tacet
　　　　　　　　　　　　Cadd9　　　　　　　　　　Gsus2　　　　　　　　　Am　　Am7

_____　I'm think-ing　it　o　-　ver　　an　-　y　-　way, _____　yeah,　yeah,　yeah. _____　Oh. __

Gtr. 4

Fmaj9/C

Gtr. 1

Gtr. 4

Gtr. 2

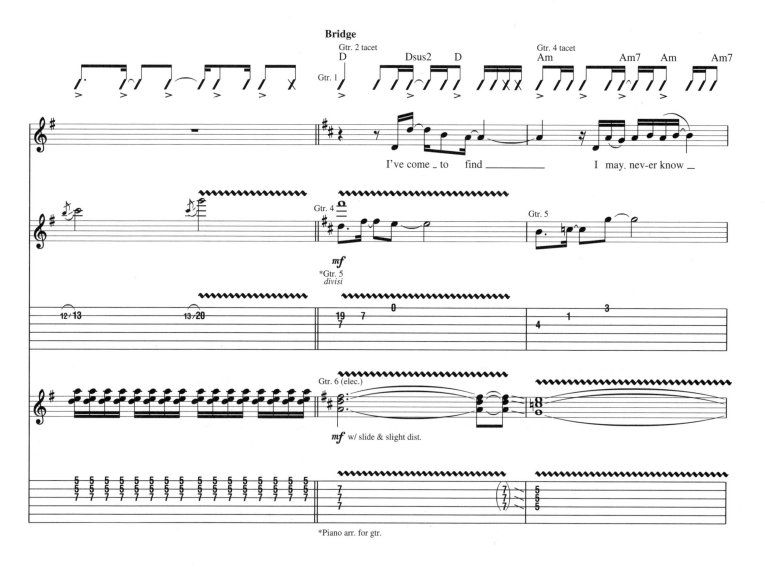

*Piano arr. for gtr.

Outro-Chorus

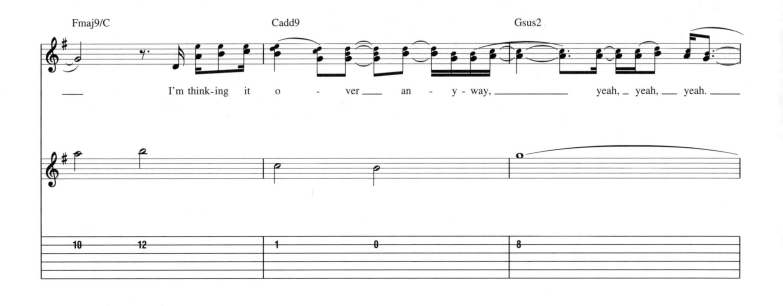

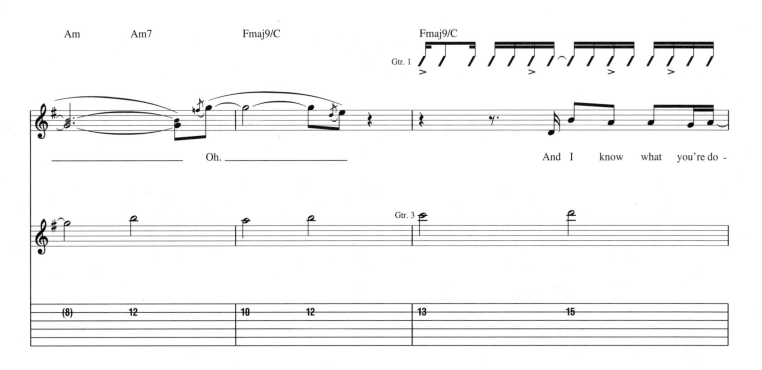

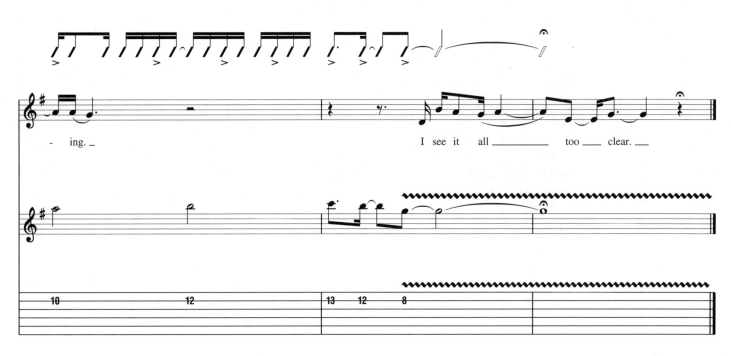

Blue on Black

Words and Music by Tia Sillers, Mark Selby and Kenny Wayne Shepherd

*Key signature denotes G Mixolydian.

32

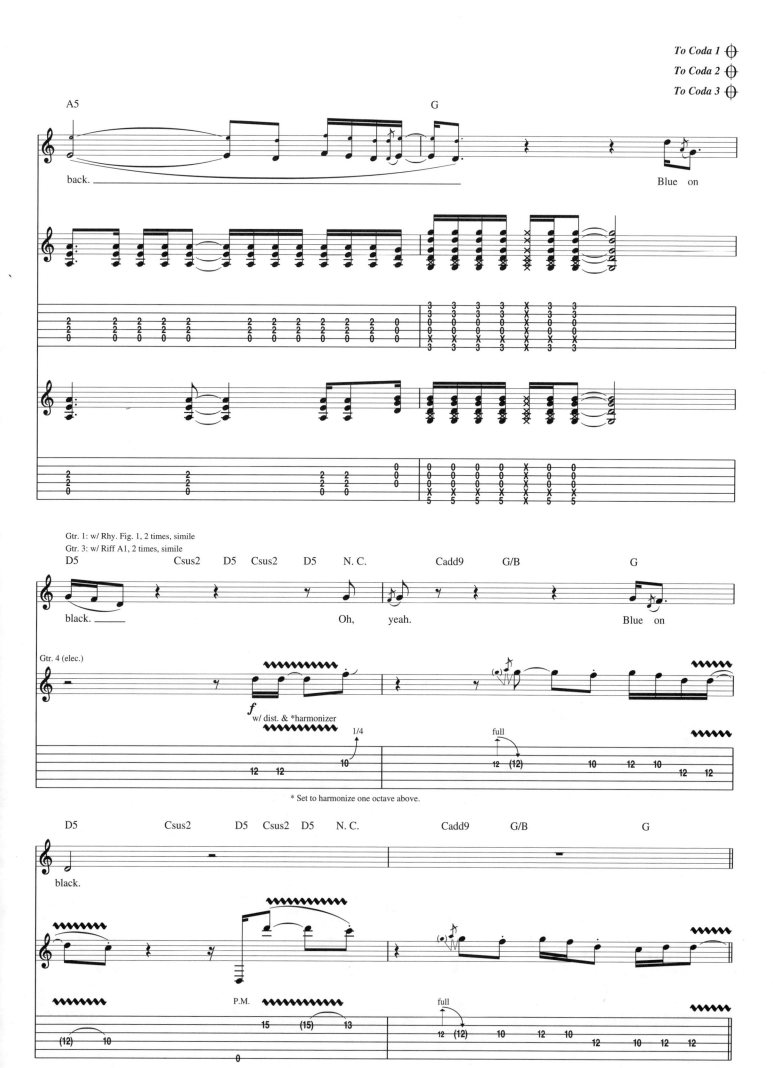

Verse

Gtr. 1: w/ Rhy. Fig. 1, 8 times, simile
Gtr. 3: w/ Riff A1, 8 times, simile

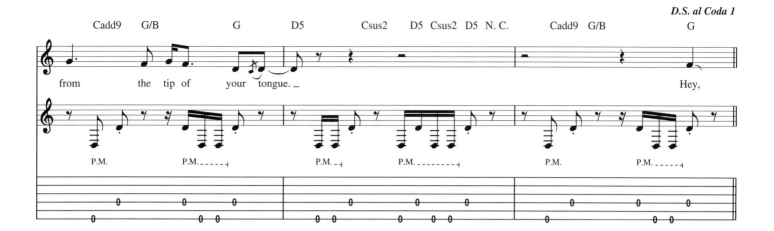

⊕ *Coda 1*

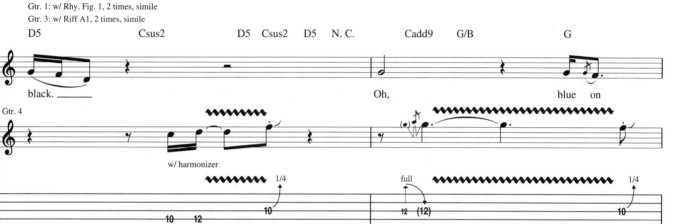

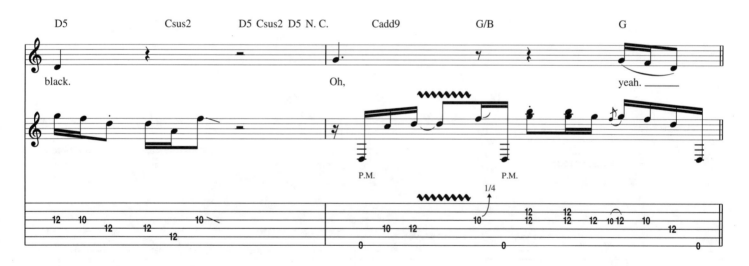

Guitar Solo

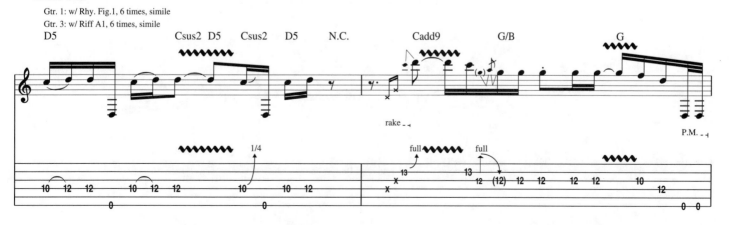

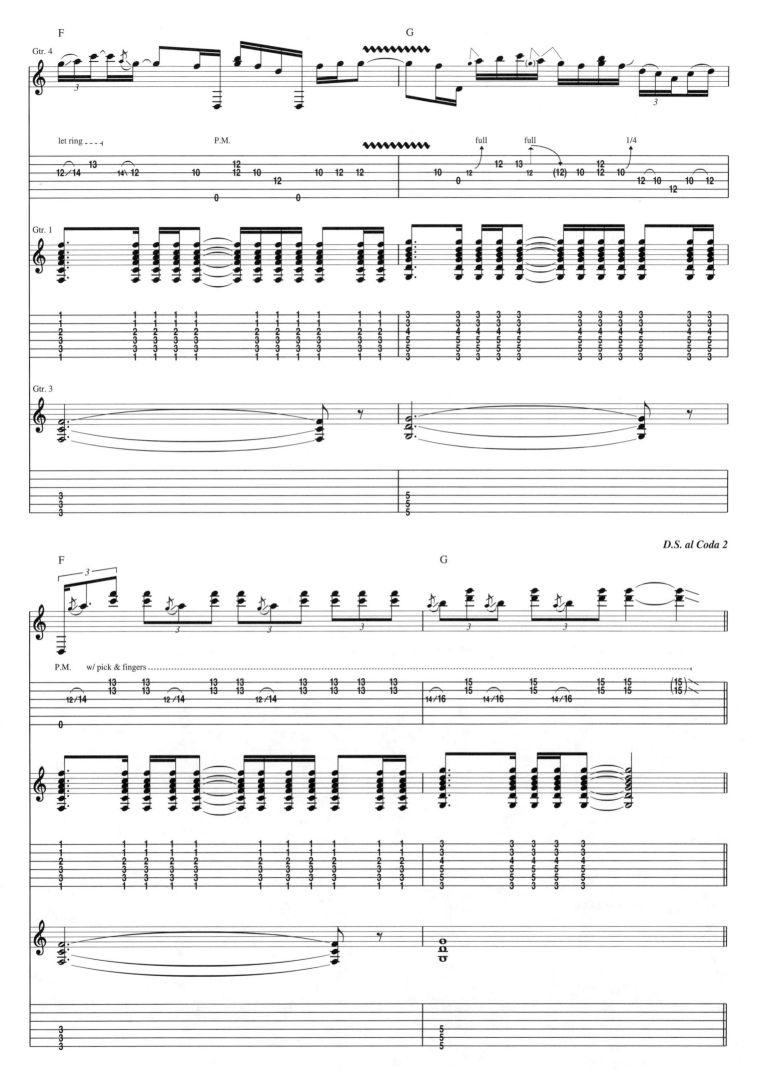

Boot Scootin' Boogie

Words and Music by Ronnie Dunn

hon - ky tonk ___ near the coun - ty line. ___ The joint starts jump - in' ev - 'ry
quit - tin' time, ___ I hit the door run - nin'. I fire up my pick - up truck

shot at that red - head yon - der look - in' at me. ___ The dance floor's hop - pin' and it's

4th time only

A

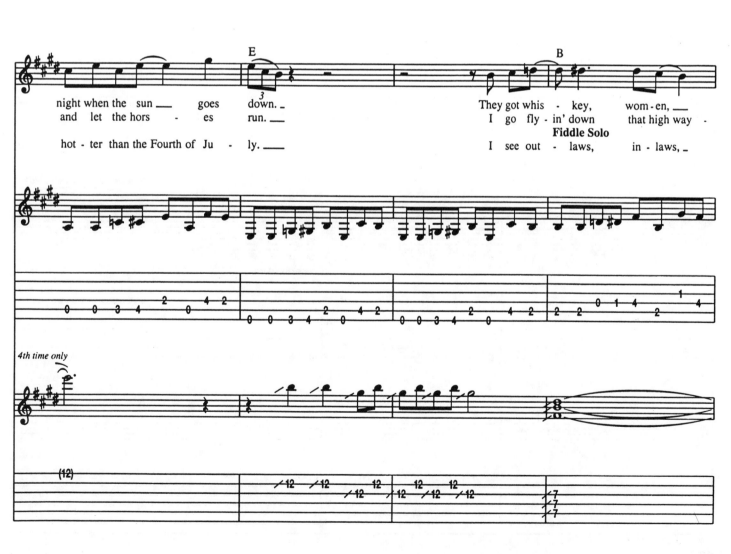

night when the sun ___ goes down. _ They got whis - key, wom - en, ___
and let the hors - es run. _ I go fly - in' down that high way -
hot - ter than the Fourth of Ju - ly. ___ I see out - laws, in - laws, _

E

B

Fiddle Solo

4th time only

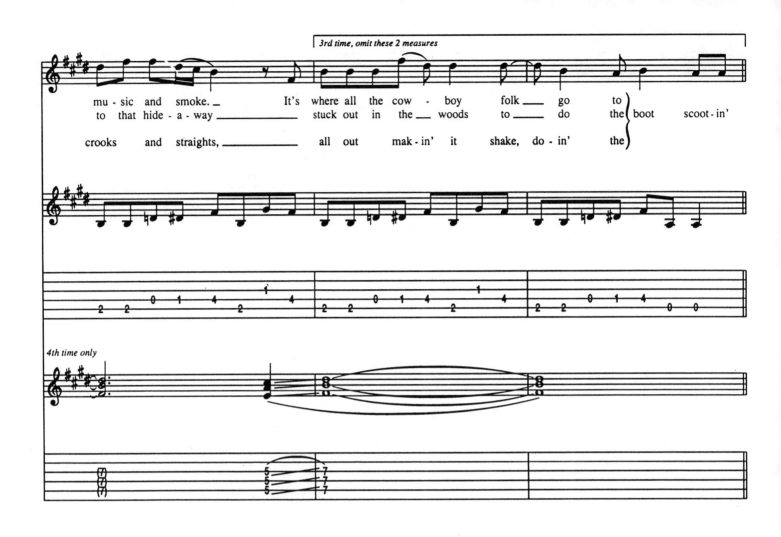

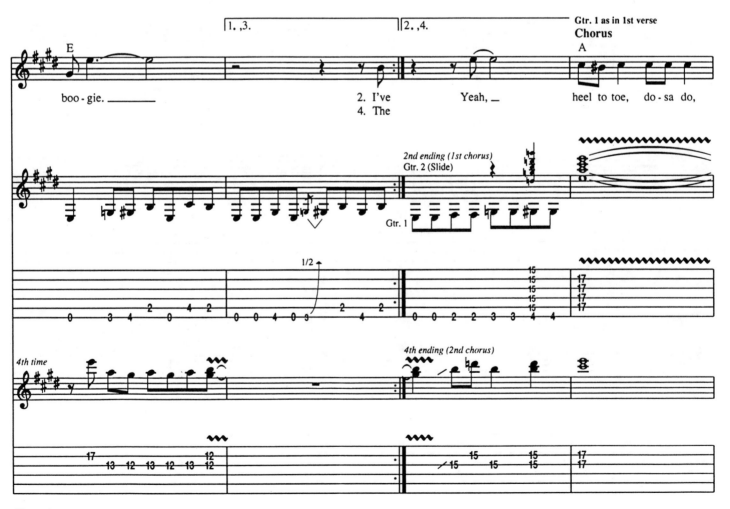

come on ba - by, let's go   boot scoot-in'!   Whoa, __   Cad - il - lac, Black-jack,

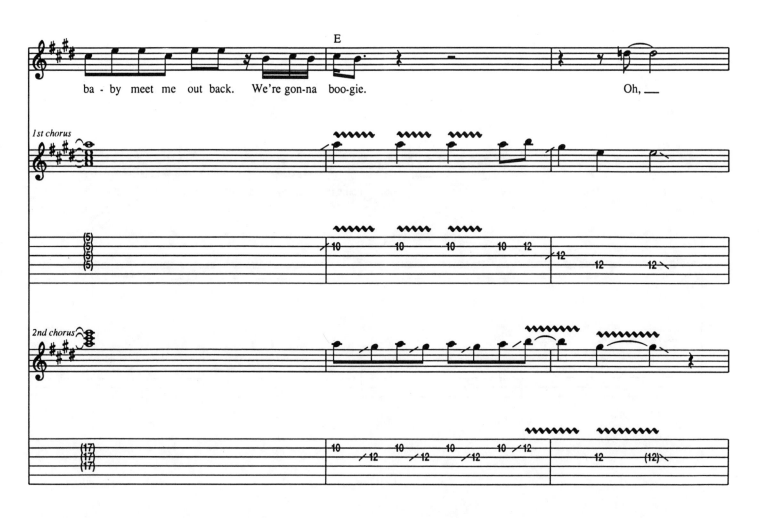

ba - by meet me out back.   We're gon-na boo-gie.   Oh, __

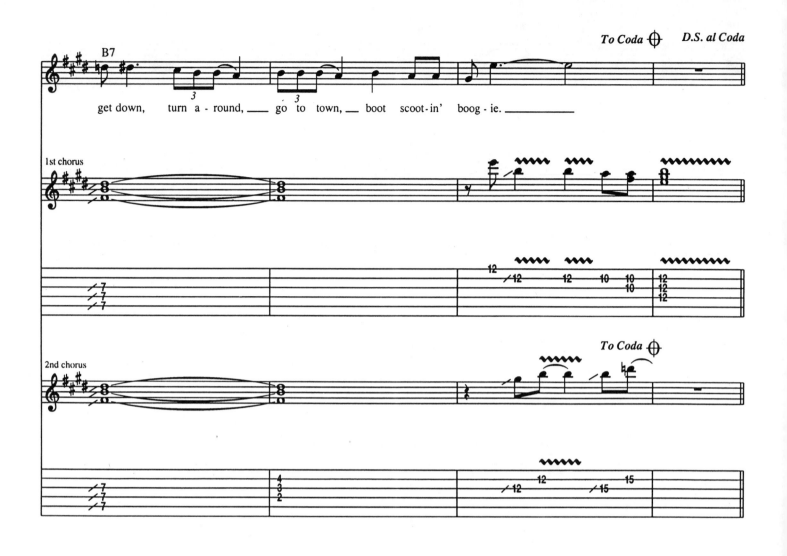

get down,   turn a - round, ___ go to town, ___ boot scoot - in' boog - ie. _____

Whoa, ___   heel to toe,   do - sa do,   come on ba - by, let's go   boot scoot - in'!

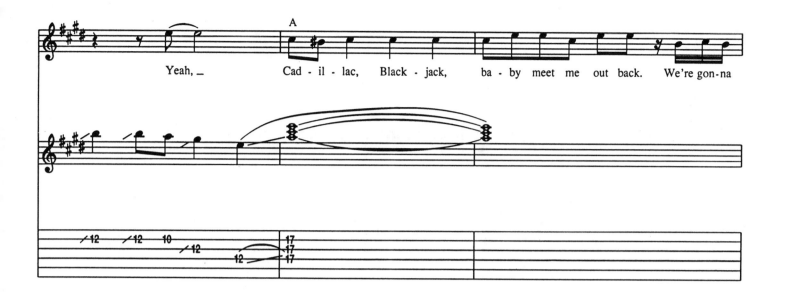

Yeah, — Cad - il - lac, Black - jack, ba - by meet me out back. We're gon-na

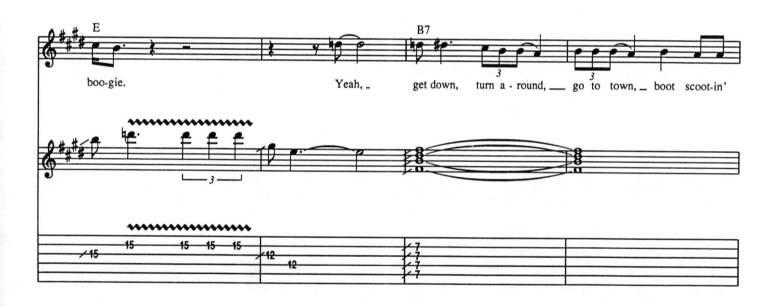

boo-gie.   Yeah, —   get down,   turn a - round, — go to town, — boot scoot-in'

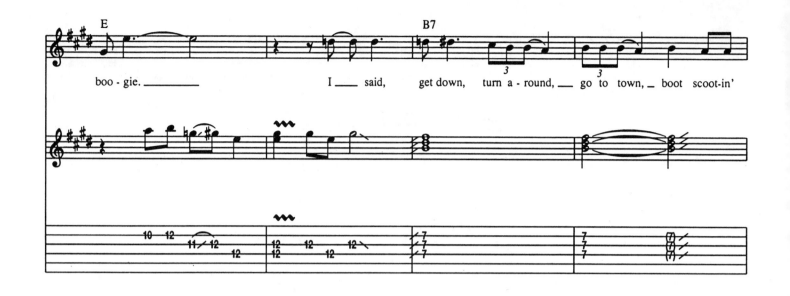

boo - gie. _____ I _____ said, get down, turn a - round, ___ go to town, _ boot scoot-in'

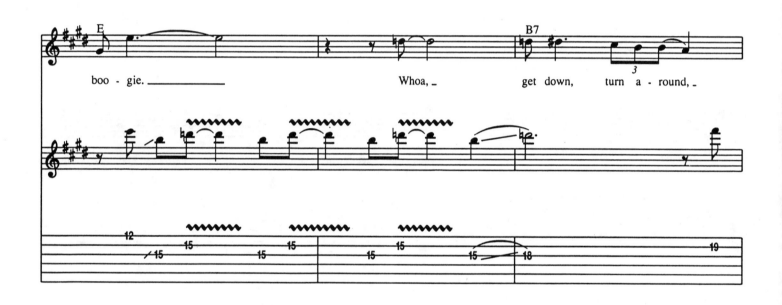

boo - gie. _____ Whoa, _ get down, turn a - round, _

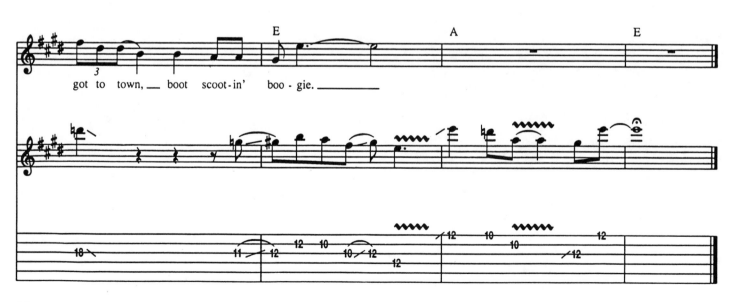

got to town, _ boot scoot-in' boo - gie. _____

Building a Mystery

Words and Music by Sarah McLachlan and Pierre Marchand

Verse

Guitar Solo

(Oo, oh, oo.

Oo. Ah, Ah.)

Oo, you're work-ing, build-ing _ a mys-ter - y.

*quick vol. swell

*vol. swells, backwards guitar arranged for guitar next 4 meas.

Outro-Chorus

57

Bulls on Parade

Written and Arranged by Rage Against The Machine

That rot-ten sore on tha face of Moth-er Earth gets big-ger. Tha trig-ger's cold, emp-ty ya purse.
arms ware - hous-es fill as quick as tha cells.
Ral - ly 'round tha fam - ly, pock-et full of shells.

Chorus

N.C.

Ral - ly 'round tha ___ fam-'ly with a pock-et full of shells. They

Gtr. 1

Rhy. Fig. 2

wah-wah off

ral - ly 'round the ___ fam-'ly with a pock-et full of shells. They

End Rhy. Fig. 2

Gtr. 1: w/ Rhy. Fig. 2

ral - ly 'round the ___ fam-'ly with a pock-et full of shells. They

1.

ral - ly 'round the _ fam-'ly with a pock-et full of shells.

2.

pock-et full of shells.

Interlude

B5

play 3 times

Bulls on pa-rade!

Gtrs. 1 & 2 +> o <+> o <+> o <+> o <+> o <+> o <+> o   <+> o <+> o <+> o <+> o <+> o <+>

w/ wah-wah

Guitar Solo

Gtr. 2 tacet
N.C.

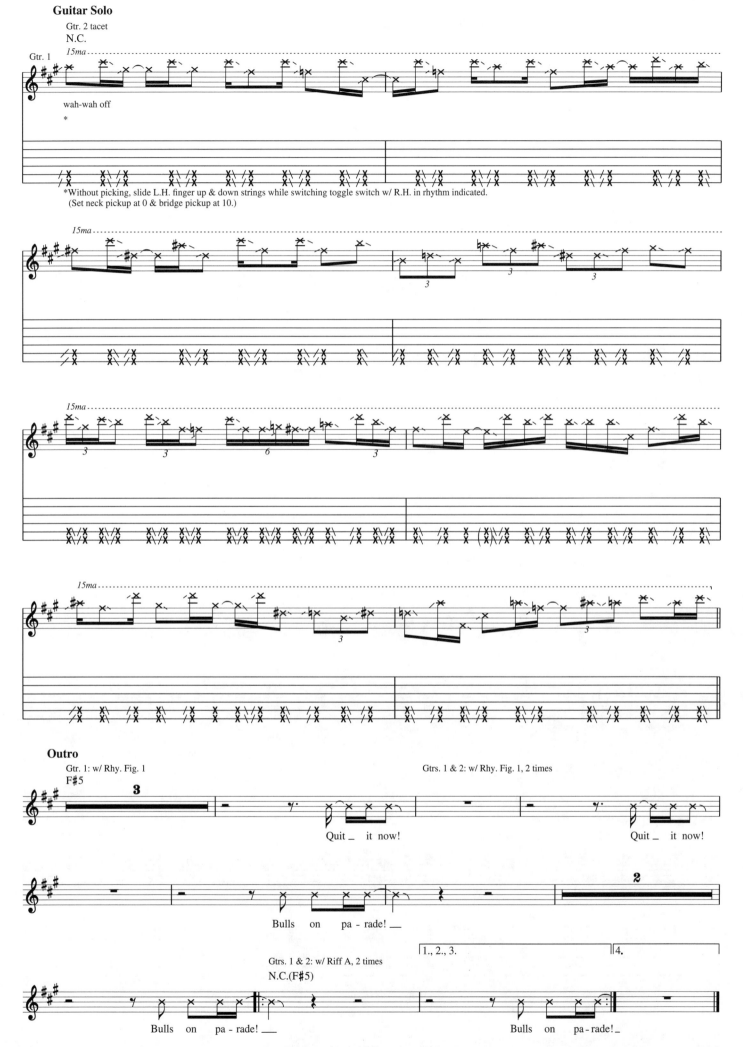

*Without picking, slide L.H. finger up & down strings while switching toggle switch w/ R.H. in rhythm indicated.
(Set neck pickup at 0 & bridge pickup at 10.)

Outro

Gtr. 1: w/ Rhy. Fig. 1

Gtrs. 1 & 2: w/ Rhy. Fig. 1, 2 times

F#5

Quit _ it now!   Quit _ it now!

Bulls   on   pa - rade! __

Gtrs. 1 & 2: w/ Riff A, 2 times
N.C.(F#5)

1., 2., 3.   4.

Bulls   on   pa - rade! __   Bulls   on   pa - rade! _

Come Out and Play

Words and Music by Dexter Holland

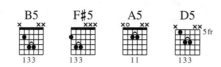

Intro

Moderately Fast Rock ♩ = 158

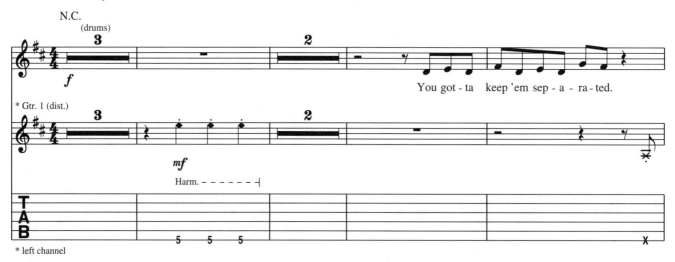

You got - ta keep 'em sep - a - ra - ted.

* Gtr. 1 (dist.)

mf

Harm. - - - - - -

* left channel

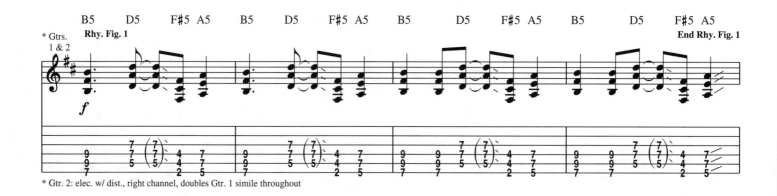

* Gtr. 2: elec. w/ dist., right channel, doubles Gtr. 1 simile throughout

Gtrs. 1 & 2: w/ Rhy. Fig. 1, simile

Gtr. 3 (dist.)

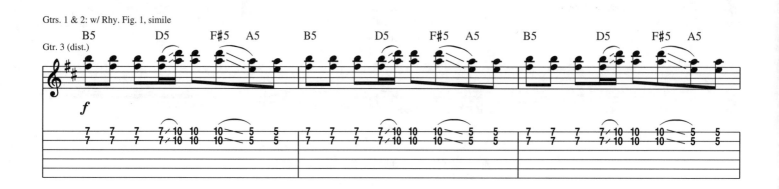

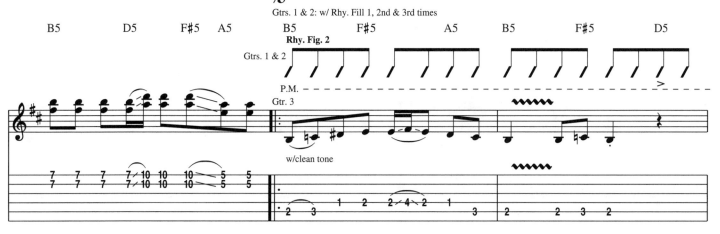

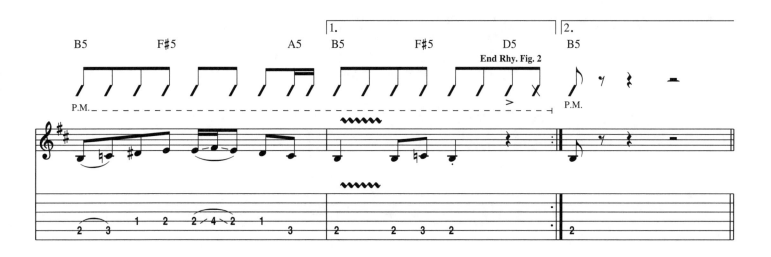

Verse

Gtr. 3 tacet

1. Like the lat - est fash - ion, like a spread-ing dis - ease.
2. By the time you hear the si - ren it's al - read - y too late.

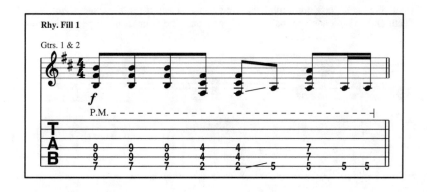

Chorus

1. Hey, man you talk-in' back to me?
2. Hey, man you dis - re-spect-ing me?

Take him out. You got - ta keep 'em sep - a - ra - ted.

Gtrs. 1 & 2

Hey, _____ (they) don't pay no mind. If you're un - der eigh - teen you won't be do - ing an - y time. _____

(3rd time) To Coda 2 ⊕

To Coda 1 ⊕
D.S. al Coda 1

Hey, _____ come out and play. _____

⊕ *Coda 1*

Interlude
Gtrs. 1 & 2: w/ Rhy. Fig. 2, simile

Gtr. 3

w/clean tone

2nd time, D.S.S. al Coda 2 ⊕ *Coda 2*

Gtrs.
1 & 2

Cryin'

Words and Music by Steven Tyler, Joe Perry and Taylor Rhodes

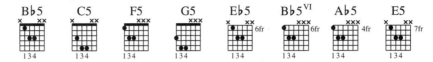

Intro
Moderately Slow Rock ♩. = 70

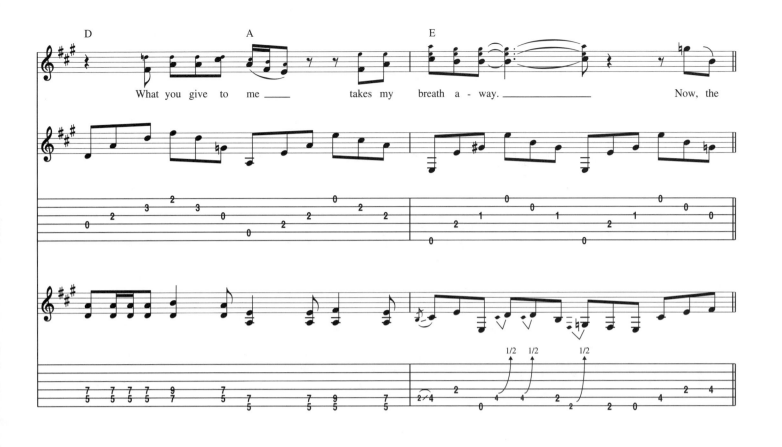

What you give to me ____ takes my breath a - way. _____ Now, the

Pre-Chorus

word out on the street _ is the dev - il's in your kiss. If our love goes up in flames, it's a

Chorus

fire I ___ can't re - sist. ____ I was cry - in' _ when I met you. Now I'm try - in' to for - get you. ____

Your love is sweet mis-er-y. I was cry-in' just to get you. Now I'm

dy-in' cause I let you do what you do to me. Yeah!

Guitar Solo

Gtrs. 2 & 3: w/ Rhy. Figs. 1 & 1A, 1st 3 meas. only

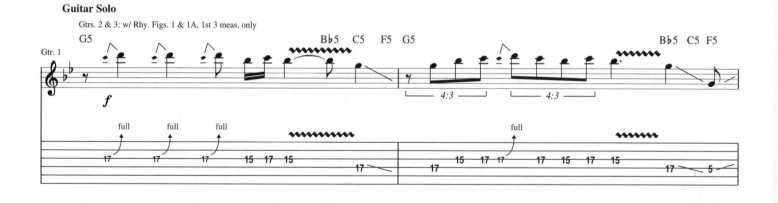

'Cause what you got in - side ain't

where your love should stay. Yeah, our love, sweet love, ain't love till you

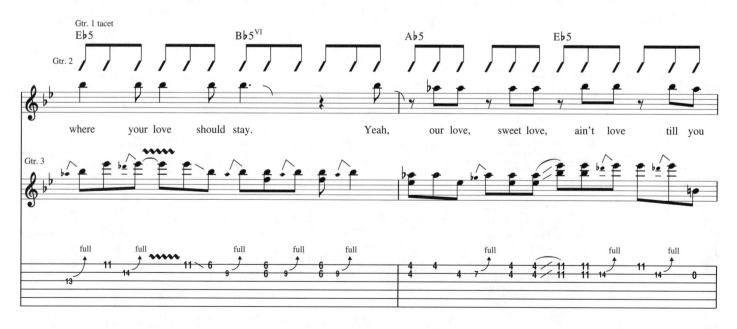

do what you, do what you do down to me, ba-by, ba-by, ba-by, ba-by, ba-by, ba-by.

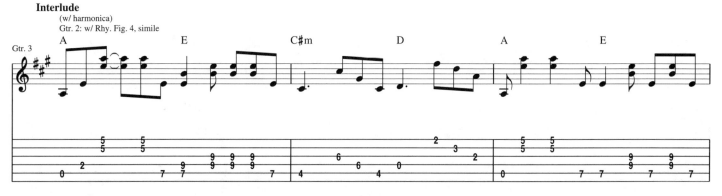

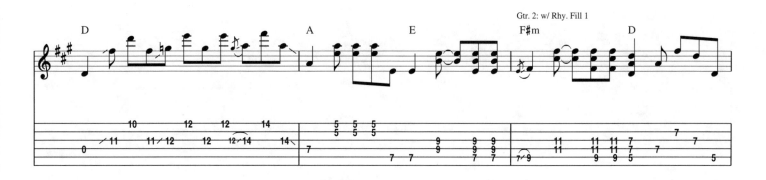

76

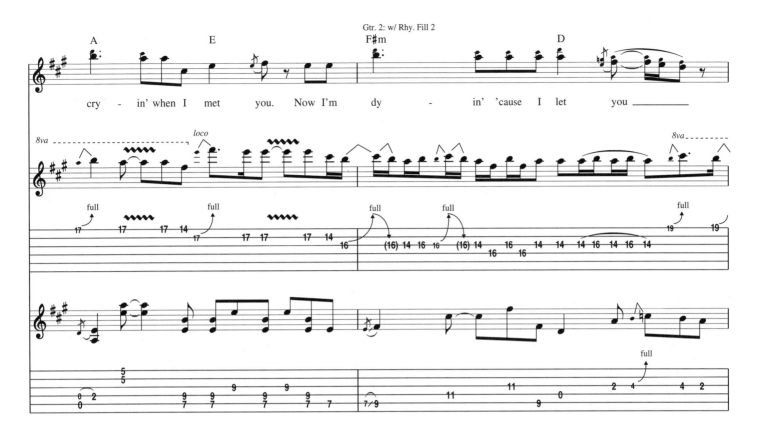

cry - in' when I met you. Now I'm dy - in' 'cause I let you _____

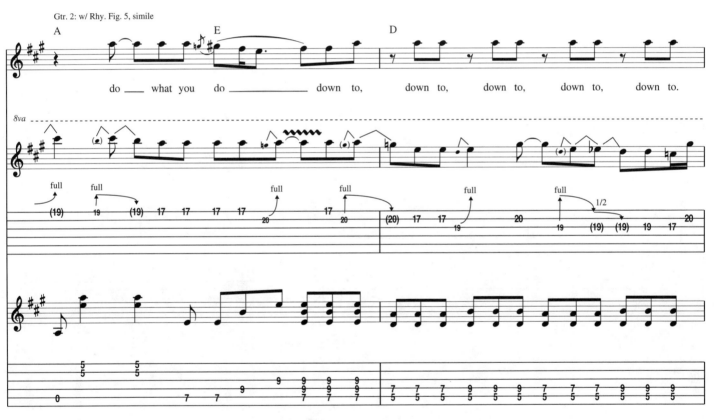

do ___ what you do _____ down to, down to, down to, down to, down to.

Begin Fade

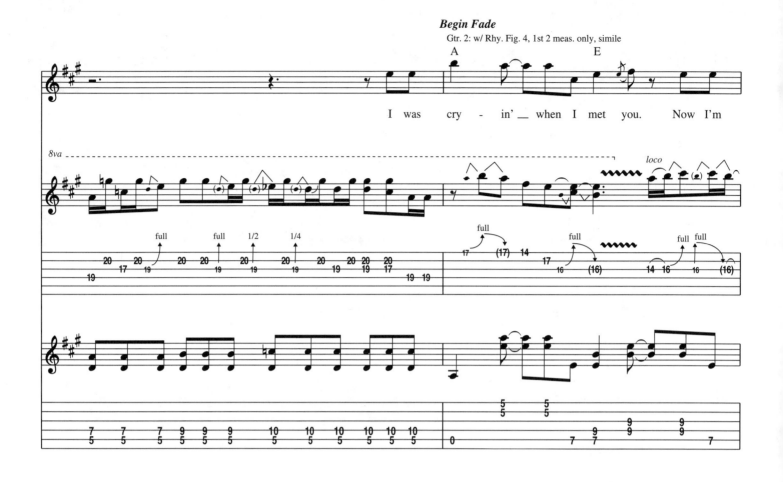

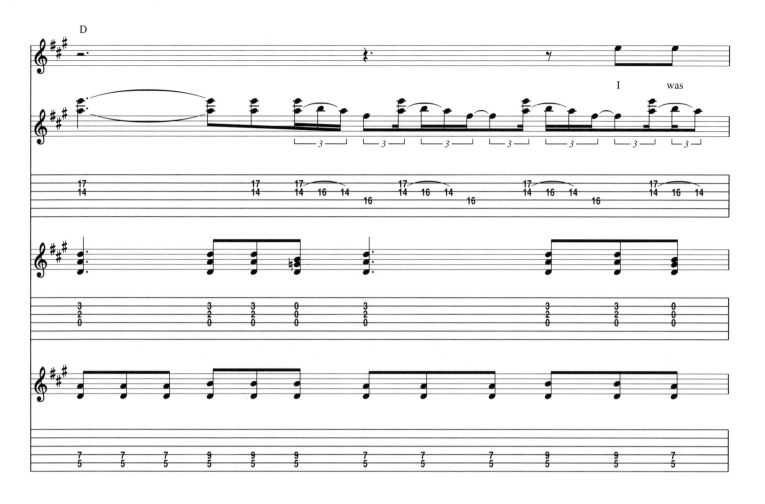

(Everything I Do) I Do It for You

Words and Music by Bryan Adams, Robert John Lange and Michael Kamen

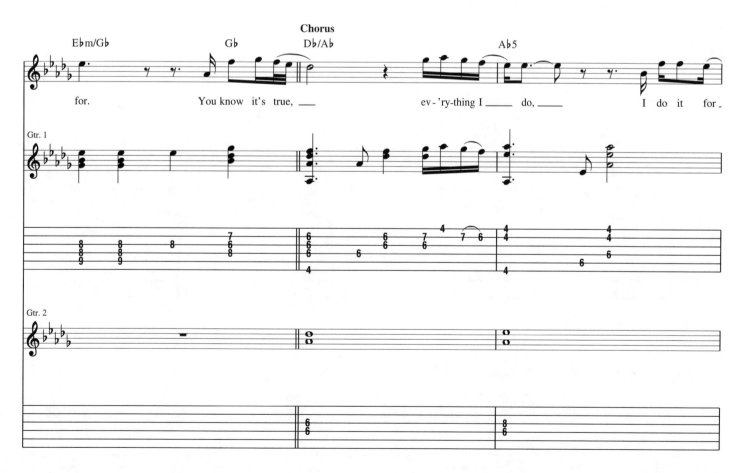

82

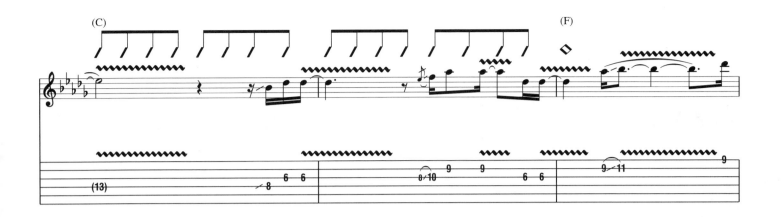

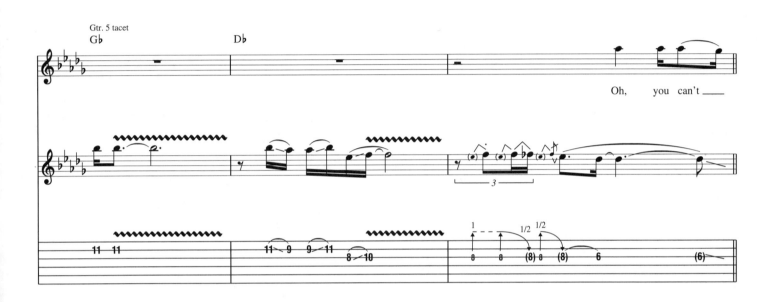

Pre-Chorus

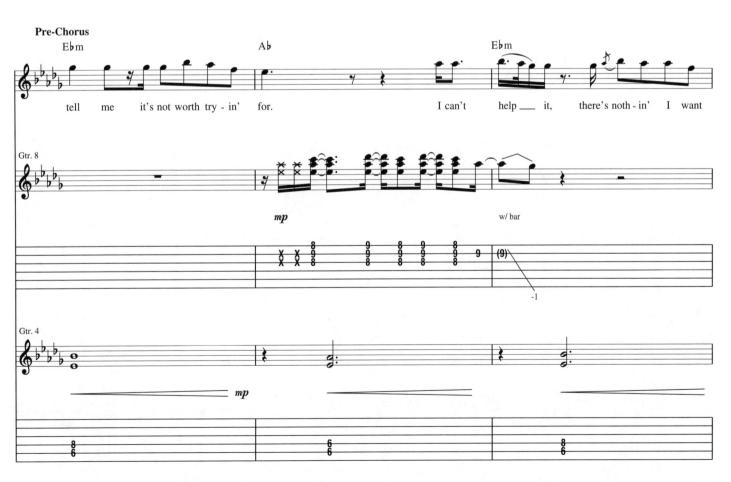

more. _____ Yeah, _ I would fight _ for you, I'd lie _____ for you, walk the

wire for you. Yeah, _ I'd die for ___ you. _____ You know it's

86

Fields of Gold

Written and Composed by Sting

*Chord symbols in parentheses reflect overall tonality.

Free As a Bird

Words and Music by John Lennon, Paul McCartney, George Harrison and Ringo Starr

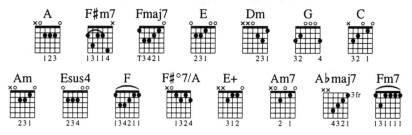

Gtr. 2; Tune High E Down 1 Step:

① = D   ④ = D
② = B   ⑤ = A
③ = G   ⑥ = E

Intro

Moderately Slow ♩ = 72

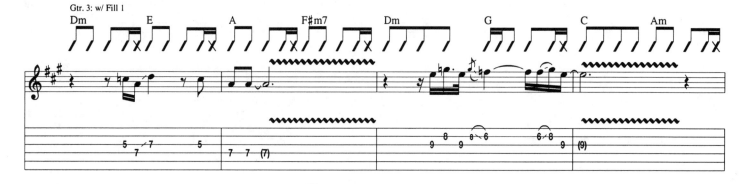

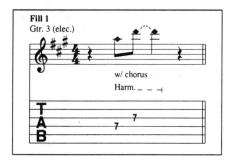

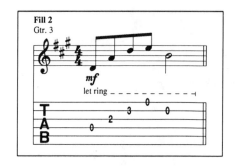

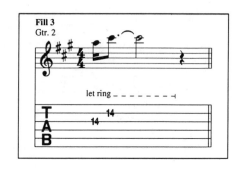

To Coda ⊕

Gtr. 3: w/ Fill 2

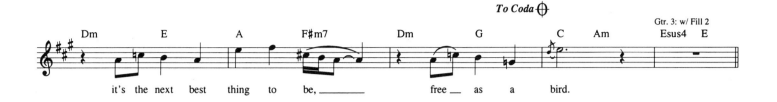

it's the next best thing to be, _____ free __ as a bird.

Verse

Gtr. 1: w/ Rhy. Fig. 1, simile

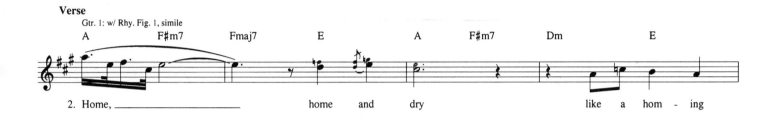

2. Home, _____ home and dry _____ like a hom - ing

Gtr. 3: w/ Fill 2

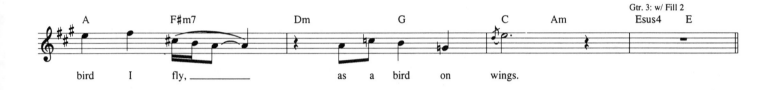

bird I fly, _____ as a bird on wings.

Bridge

Gtr. 1

What - ev - er hap-pened to ___ the life that we once knew?

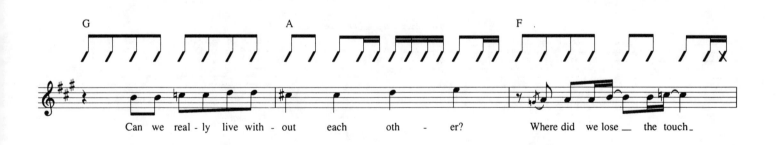

Can we real - ly live with - out each oth - er? Where did we lose __ the touch__

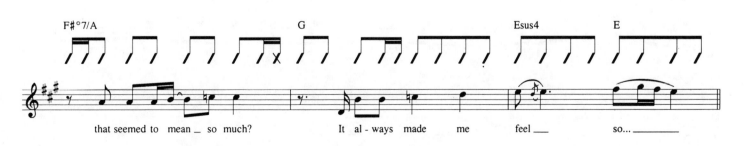

that seemed to mean __ so much? It al - ways made me feel ___ so... _____

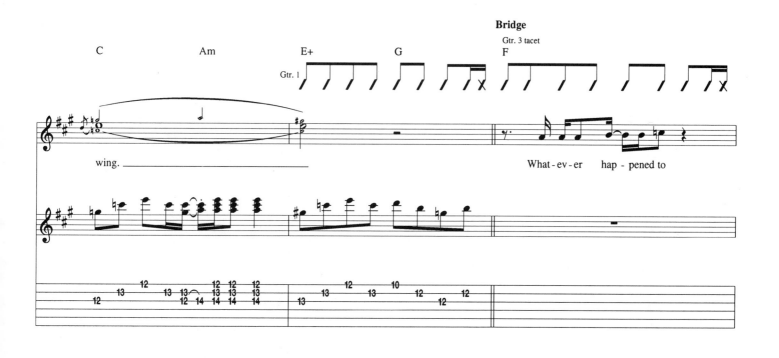

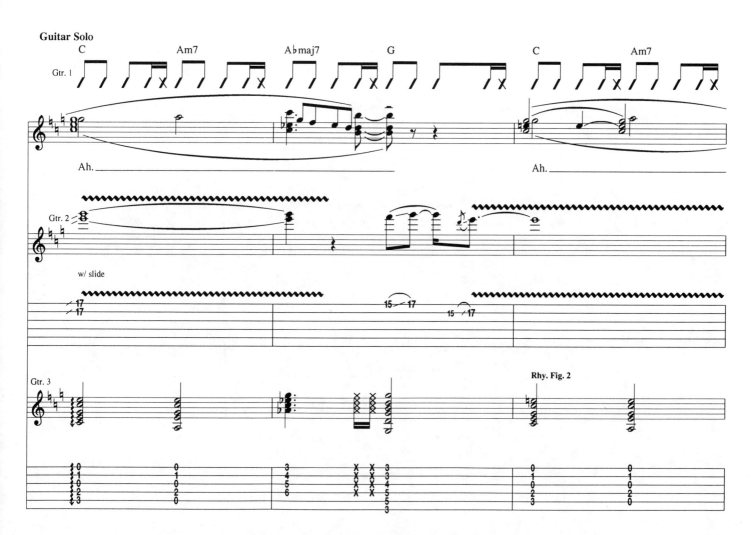

* Play between 5th & 6th frets.

Friends in Low Places

Words and Music by Dewayne Blackwell and Earl Bud Lee

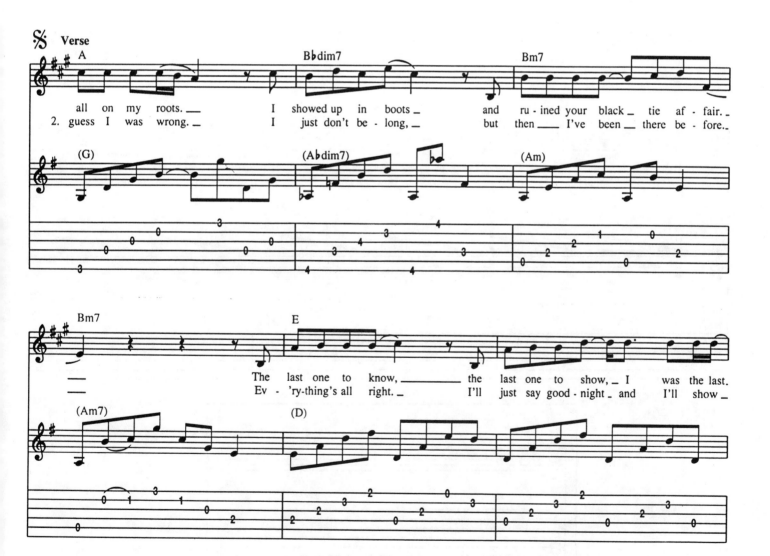

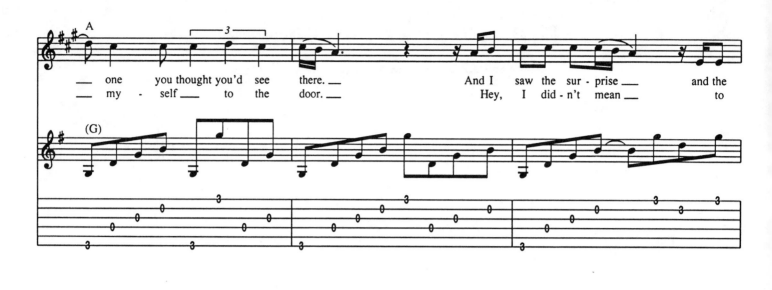

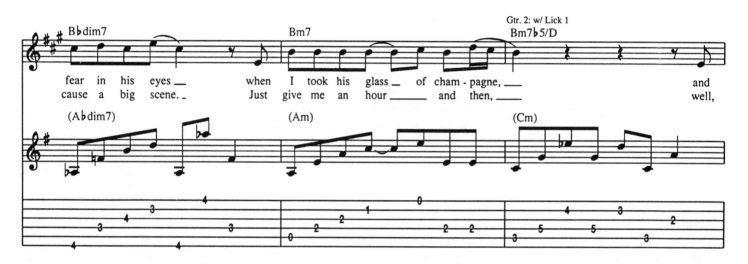

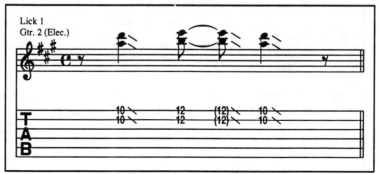

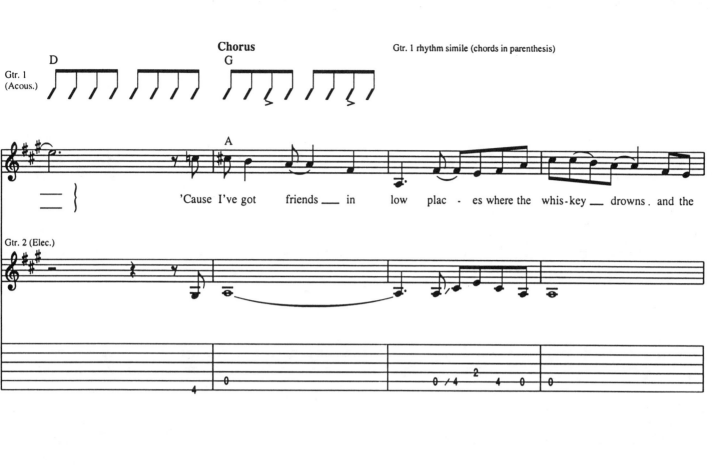

'Cause I've got friends ___ in low plac - es where the whis-key ___ drowns . and the

beer ___ chas - es my blues ___ a-way, and I'll be o - kay. ___

Yeah, I'm not big ___ on so - cial gra - ces. Think I'll slip on ___ down ___ to the

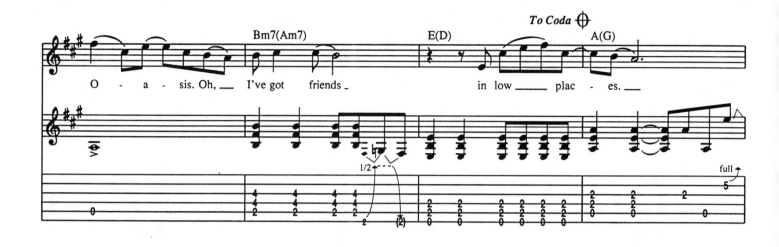

O - a - sis. Oh, ___ I've got friends ___ in low ___ plac - es. ___

D.S. al Coda

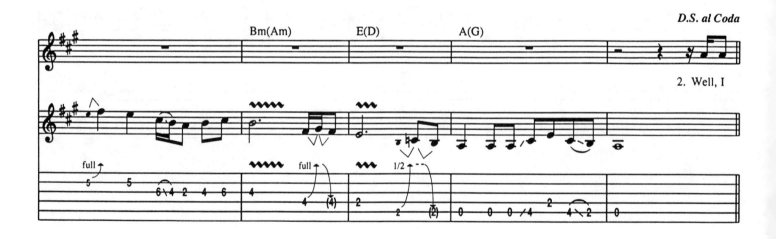

2. Well, I

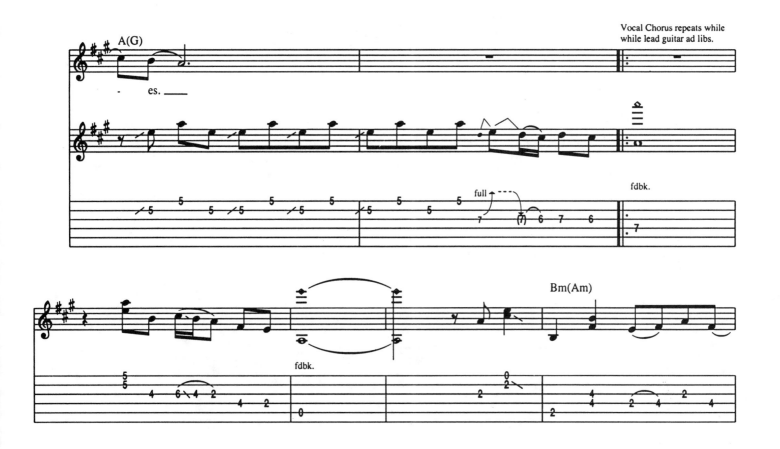

Vocal Chorus repeats while
while lead guitar ad libs.

Repeat Ad Lib. Guitar and Fade

Give Me One Reason

Words and Music by Tracy Chapman

Guitar Solo

5. This youth-ful heart can love you, ____ yes, and give you what you need. _____

I said this youth-ful heart can love you, ____ ho, and give you what you need. _____

But I'm too old to go chas-in' you a-round, _ wast-in' my pre-cious en-er-gy. _

Verse

Gtr. 1: w/ Rhy. Fig. 1

6. Give me one rea-son to stay here, _ yes, now turn right back a-round. (A -

round. _ You can see the turn in me.) Give me one rea-son to stay here _

oh, I'll turn right back a - round. _ Said I
(You can see the turn in me.)

Gtr. 2 tacet

don't wan-na leave you lone-ly, _ you _ got to make me change my

Hold My Hand

Words and Music by Darius Carlos Rucker, Everett Dean Felber, Mark William Bryan and James George Sonefeld

Gtr. 3: w/ Rhy. Fig. 4A, 2 times

B   E   F#   F#sus4   F#   F#sus4

_____
(Hold   my   hand _____)

I'll take you to a place _ where you _
I'll take you to the prom - ised

Rhy. Fig. 5   End Rhy. Fig. 5

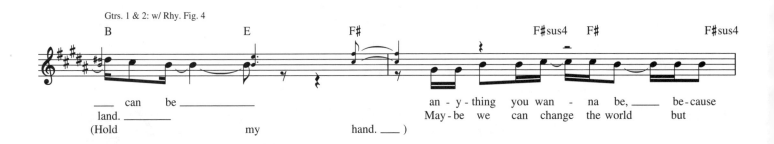

Gtrs. 1 & 2: w/ Rhy. Fig. 4

B   E   F#   F#sus4   F#   F#sus4

_____ can be _____
land. _____
(Hold   my   hand. ___)

an - y - thing you wan - na be, _____ be - cause
May - be we can change the world but

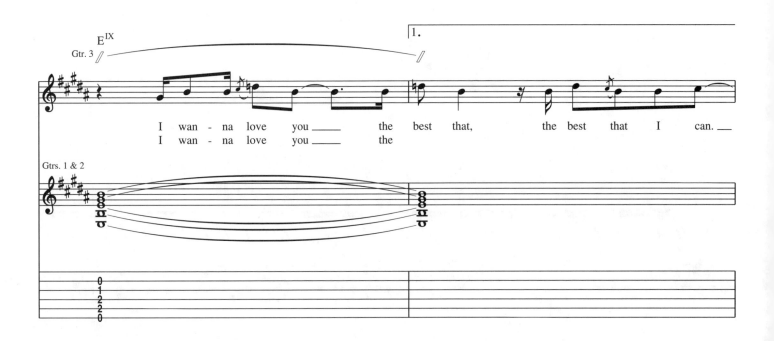

E^{IX}   1.

Gtr. 3

I wan - na love you _____ the best that, the best that I can. _
I wan - na love you _____ the

Gtrs. 1 & 2

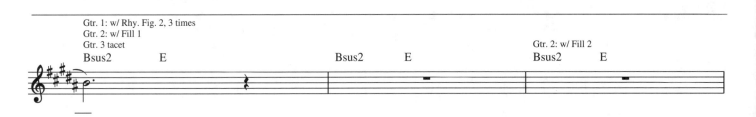

Gtr. 1: w/ Rhy. Fig. 2, 3 times
Gtr. 2: w/ Fill 1
Gtr. 3 tacet

Gtr. 2: w/ Fill 2

Bsus2   E   Bsus2   E   Bsus2   E

_____

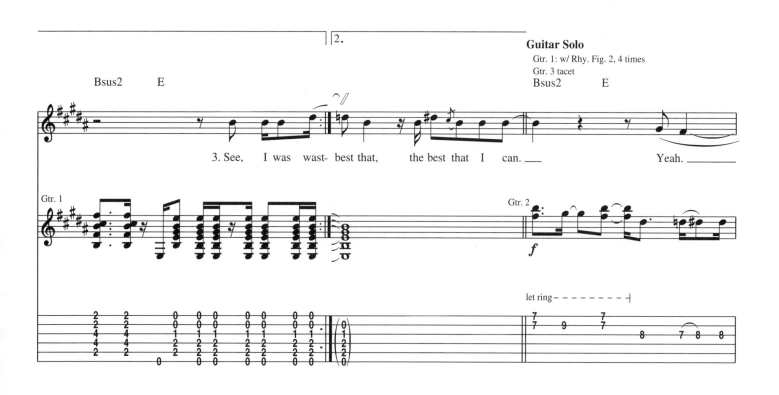

3. See,   I was   wast- best that,   the best that   I   can. ___   Yeah. ___

Oh.

Let me run, won't you _ let me run with you.

Chorus

*Gtrs. 1 & 2: w/ Rhy. Fig. 4
Gtr. 3: w/ Rhy. Fig. 4A, 3 times

Gtrs. 1 & 2: w/ Rhy. Fig. 5

(Hold   my   hand. _)

Want you   to hold   my _ hand. _____   (Hold   my   hand. _

* Gtr. 2 holds notes from end of solo for two beats, then resumes with Rhy. Fig. 4

Gtrs. 1 & 2: w/ Rhy. Fig. 4

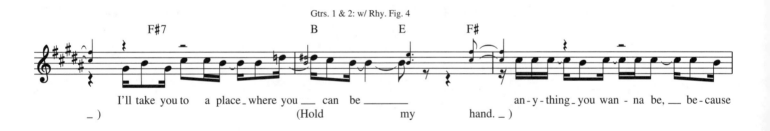

I'll take you to   a place _ where you _ can be _____   an-y-thing _ you wan - na be, _ be - cause
_)   (Hold   my   hand. _)

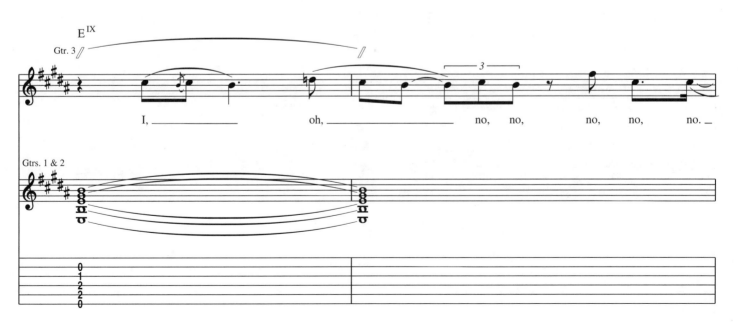

I, _____   oh, _____ no, no,   no, no,   no. _

116

I Can't Dance

Words and Music by Mike Rutherford, Phil Collins and Tony Banks

⊕ Coda

know _ who's a look-ing on. _____

A per-fect bod-y

let ring throughout

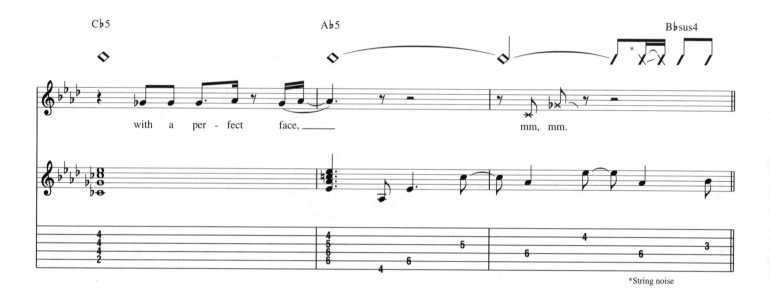

with a per-fect face, _____

mm, mm.

*String noise

Interlude
Gtr. 1: w/ Rhy. Fig. 1 (4 1/2 times)
Gtr. 2: w/ Rhy. Fig. 3 (5 times)

Outro-Chorus

No I _____ can't dance. I _____

_____ can't talk. On - ly thing a-bout me is the way I _____ walk. _____ No I _____

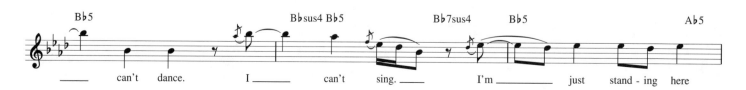

_____ can't dance. I _____ can't sing. _____ I'm _____ just stand-ing here

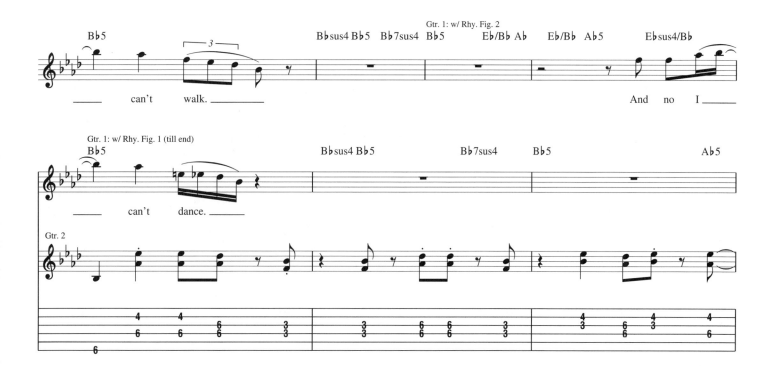

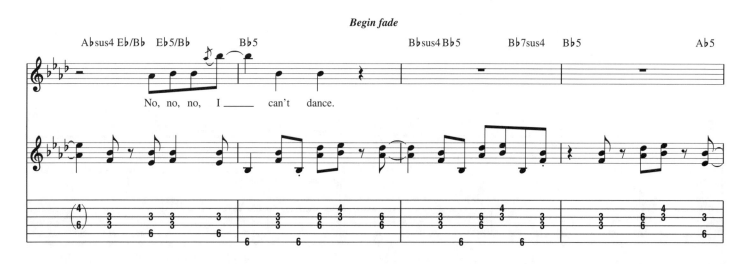

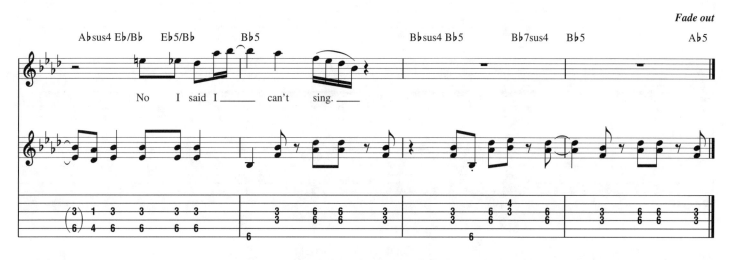

I'm the Only One

Words and Music by Melissa Etheridge

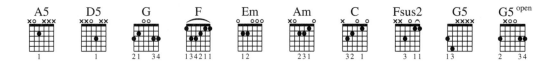

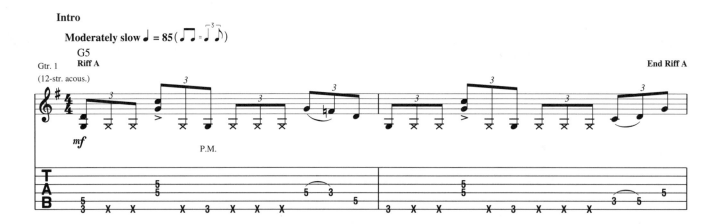

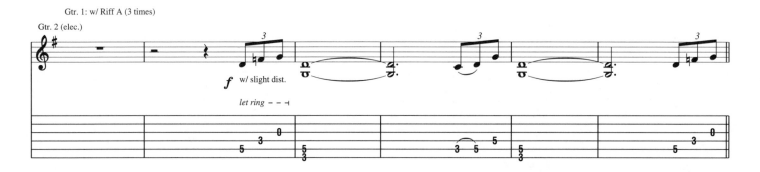

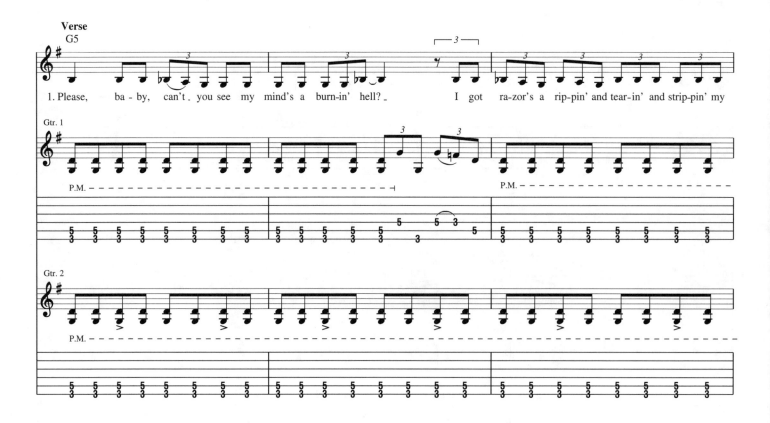

But I'm the on - ly one who'll walk a - cross a fire ___ for you. ___

And I'm the on - ly one who'll drown in my de - sire ___ for you. ___ It's

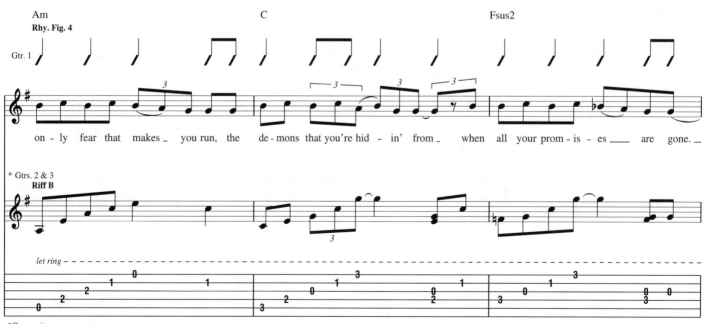

on - ly fear that makes ___ you run, the de - mons that you're hid - in' from ___ when all your prom - is - es ___ are gone. ___

*Composite arrangement.

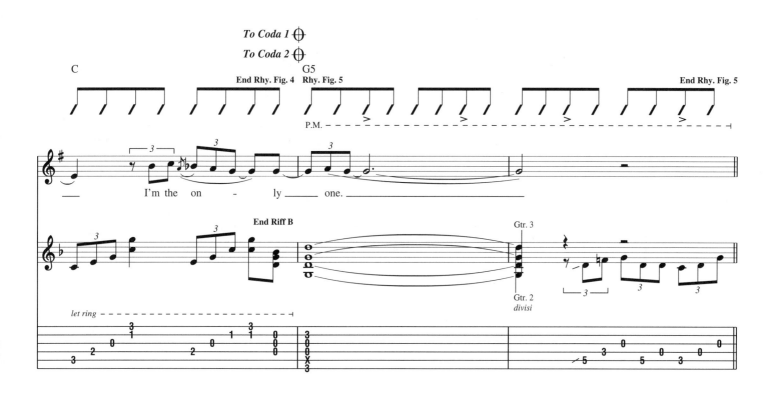

I'm the on - ly _____ one. _____

Verse

Gtr. 3 tacet
Gtr. 1: w/ Rhy. Fig. 1 (1st 2 meas. only, 2 times)

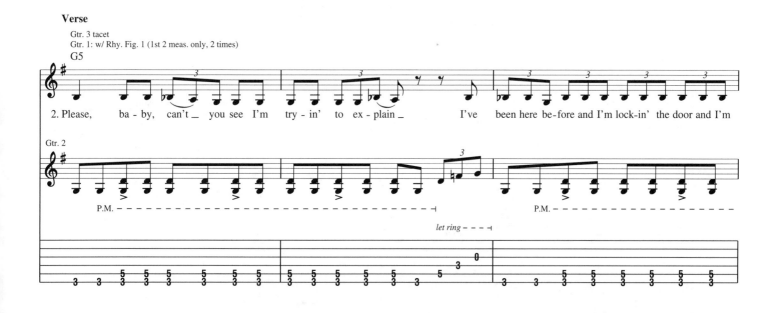

2. Please, ba - by, can't _ you see I'm try - in' to ex - plain _ I've been here be - fore and I'm lock - in' the door and I'm

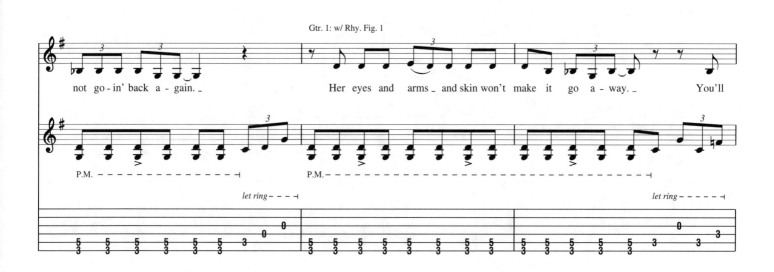

not go - in' back a - gain. _ Her eyes and arms _ and skin won't make it go a - way. _ You'll

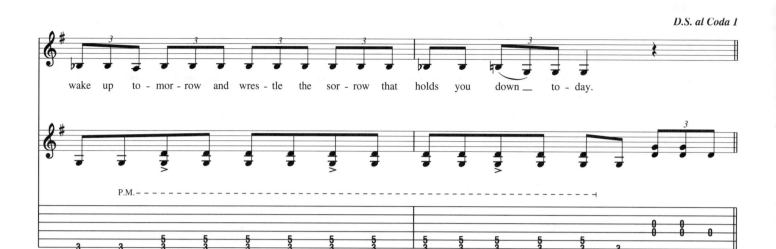

wake up to-mor-row and wres-tle the sor-row that holds you down — to-day.

$\oplus$ Coda 1

I'm the on - ly one, _ babe.

I'm the on - ly one. _

let ring

let ring

Riff C

End Riff C

mp

Begin fade

Gtr. 1: w/ Riff C (till fade)

Ain't no - bod - y else is gon - na love you,

ain't no - bod - y else _ is gon - na love _

Gtr. 2

let ring

Fade out

_ you.

Hee, hee, _____

hee, hee, hee.

let ring

let ring

The Impression That I Get

Words and Music by Dicky Barrett and Joe Gittleman

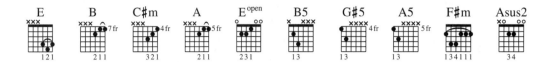

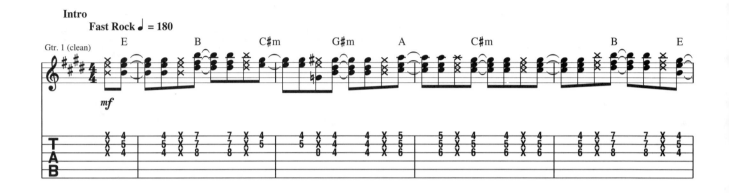

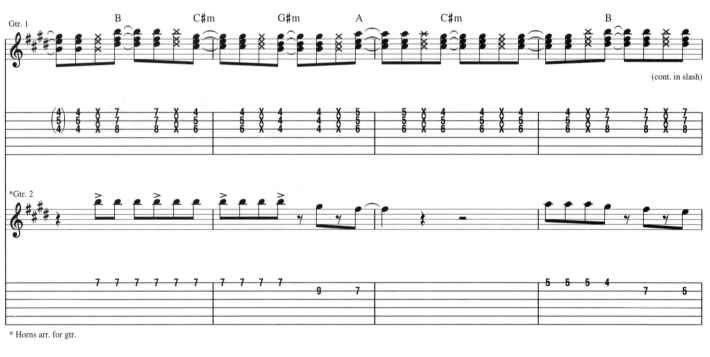

* Horns arr. for gtr.

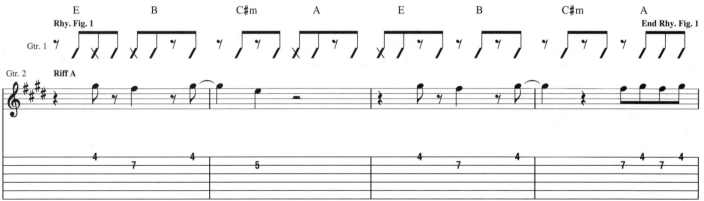

Verse

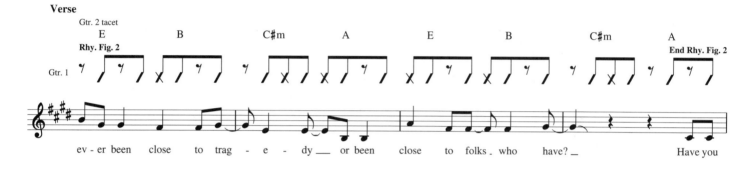

ev - er been close to trag - e - dy ___ or been close to folks ___ who have? ___ Have you

ev - er felt a pain so pow - er - ful, ___ so heav - y you ___ col - lapse? ___

Pre-Chorus

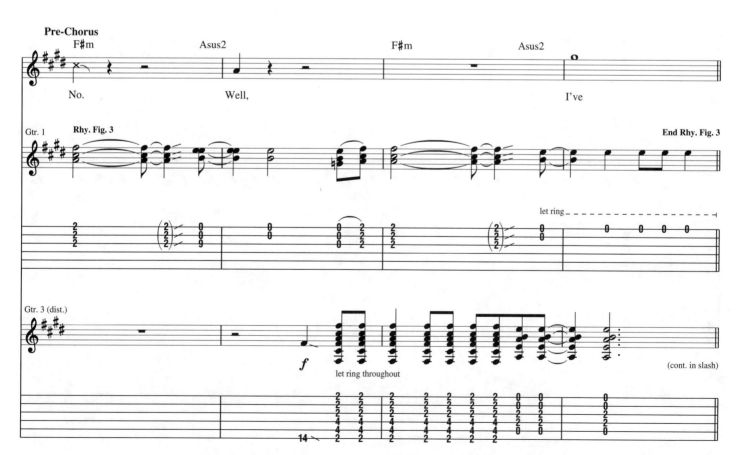

No. Well, I've

134

Look at the test-ed and think, there, but for the grace go I. Might be a cow-ard, I'm a-fraid of what I might find out.

Outro

Iris

from the Motion Picture CITY OF ANGELS

Words and Music by John Rzeznik

Gtr. 1 Tuning:
① = D ④ = D
② = D↑ ⑤ = D↓
③ = D↓ ⑥ = B↓

Intro
Moderately Slow ♩. = 51

* Two gtrs. arr. for one.
** Chord symbols reflect implied tonality.

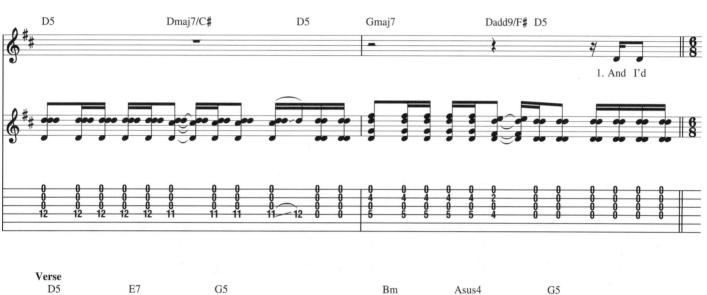

1. And I'd

Verse

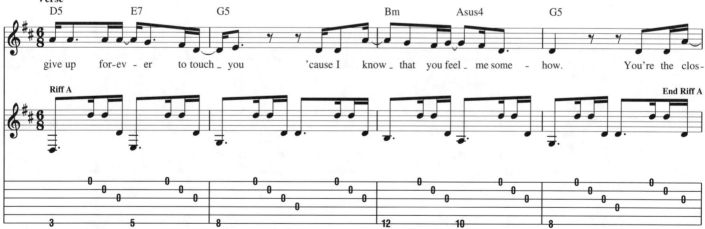

give up for-ev-er to touch _ you 'cause I know _ that you feel _ me some - how. You're the clos-

Gtr. 1: w/ Riff A, 3 times, simile

- est to heav - en that I'll ___ ev - er be, _ and I don't _ wan - na go home right now. And all _

I can taste _ is this mo-ment, and all _ I can breathe _ is your life. _ Well,

soon-er or lat-er it's o - ver, I just don't _ wan-na miss _ you to-night. _ And I

%. Chorus

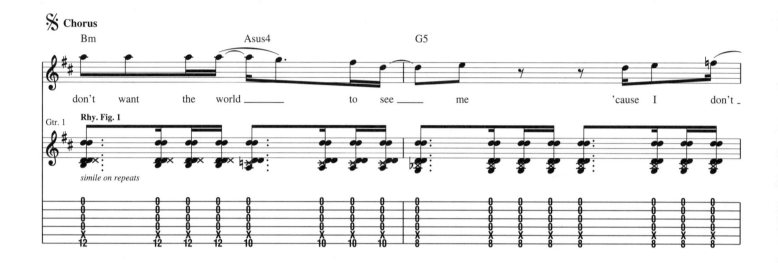

don't want the world _____ to see _____ me 'cause I don't _

Gtr. 1 Rhy. Fig. 1

simile on repeats

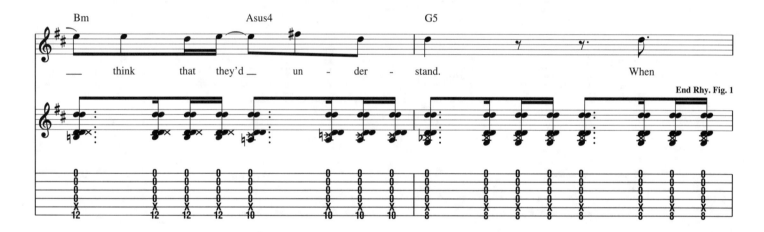

_ think that they'd _ un - der - stand. When

End Rhy. Fig. 1

To Coda 1 ⊕
To Coda 2 ⊕

Gtr. 1: w/ Rhy. Fig. 1

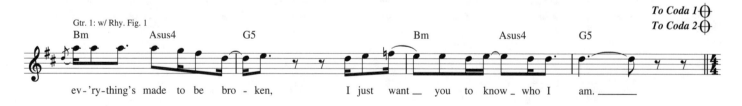

ev-'ry-thing's made to be bro - ken, I just want _ you to know _ who I am. _____

Interlude

Gtr. 1

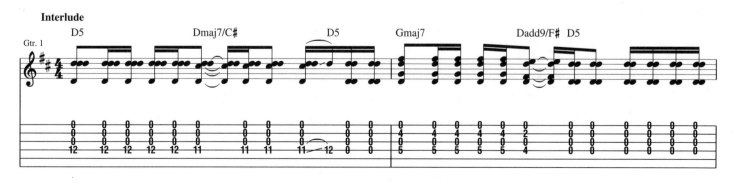

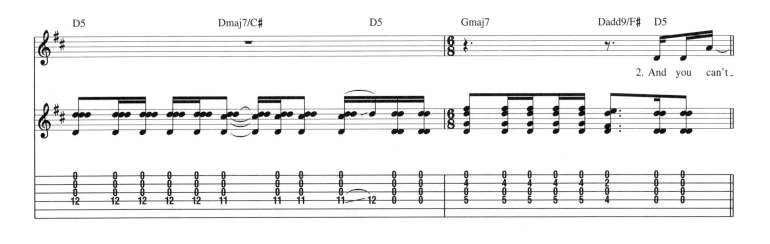

2. And you can't

Verse

Gtr. 1: w/ Riff A, 2 times, simile

___ fight the tears __ that ain't com-in' or the mo - ment of truth __ in your lies. __ When

D.S. al Coda 1

ev-'ry-thing feels like the mov - ies, yeah, you bleed __ just to know __ you're a - live. __ And I

Coda 1

Interlude

Gtr. 1

play 3 times

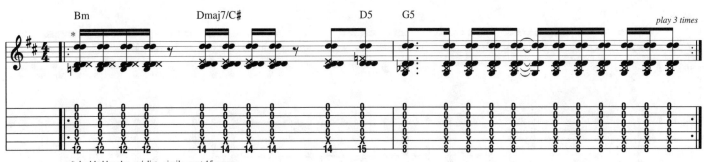

* doubled by elec. w/ dist., simile, next 15 meas.

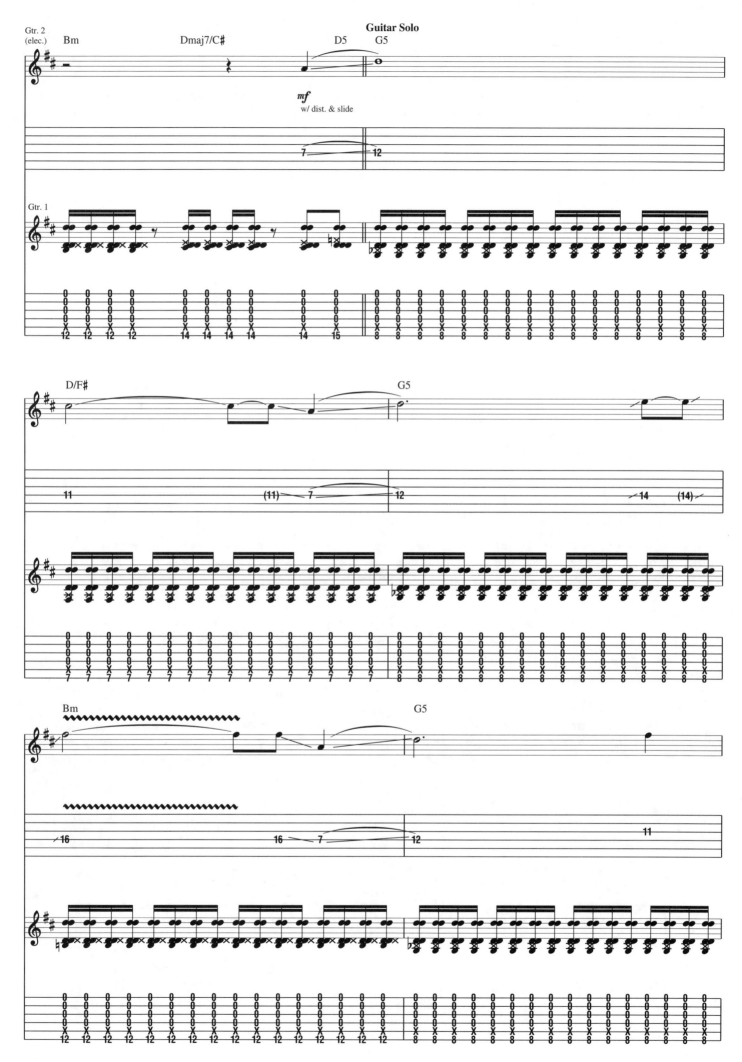

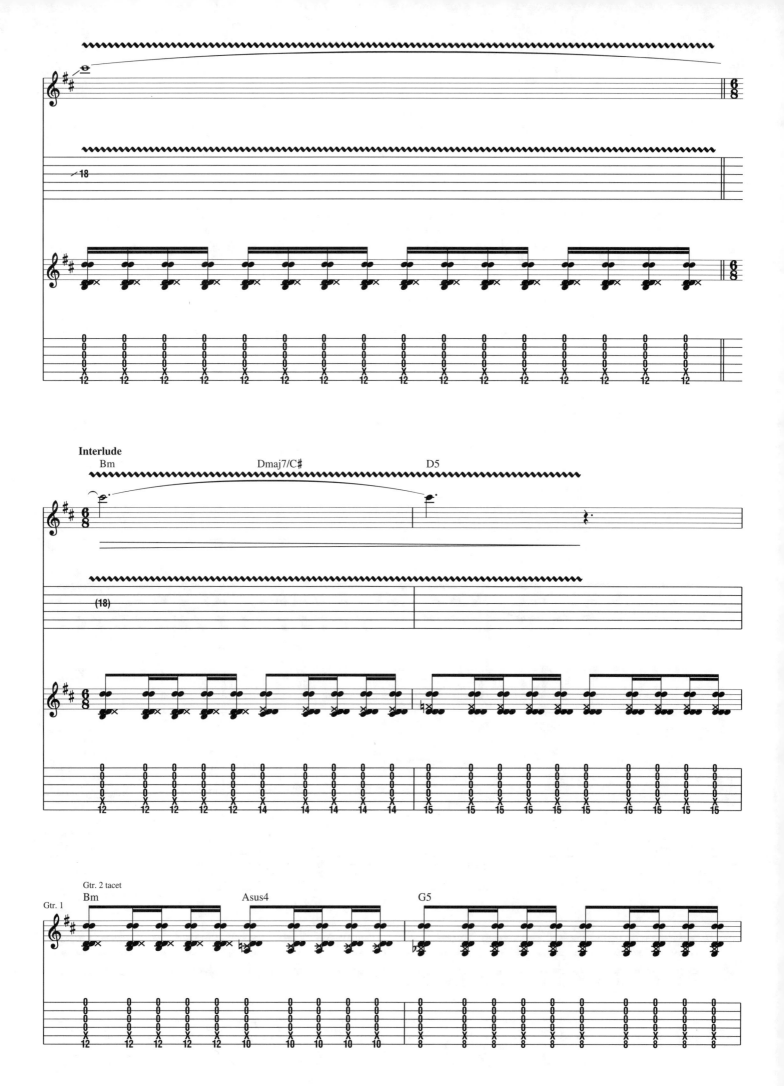

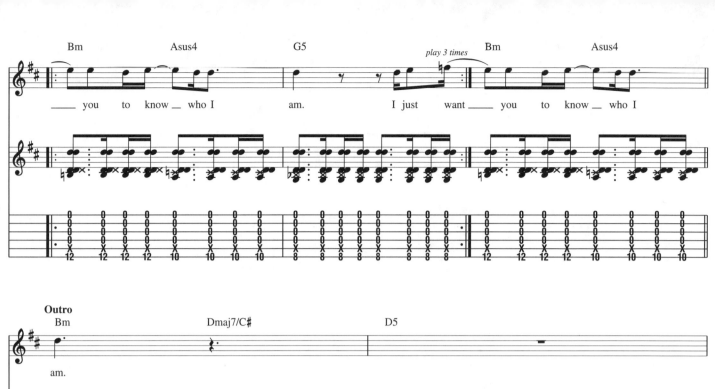

you to know __ who I am. I just want __ you to know __ who I

Outro

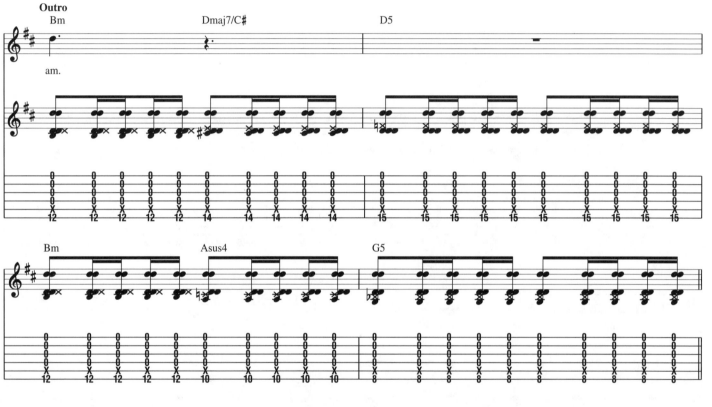

am.

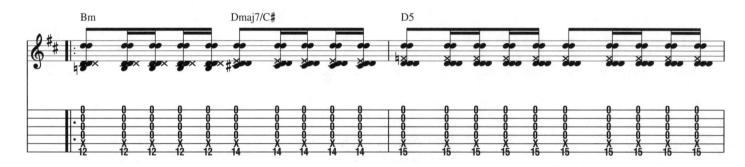

Repeat and Fade

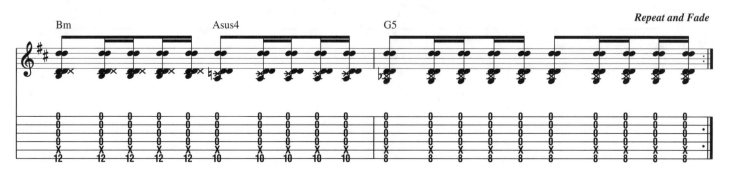

Jump, Jive an' Wail

Words and Music by Louis Prima

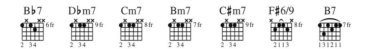

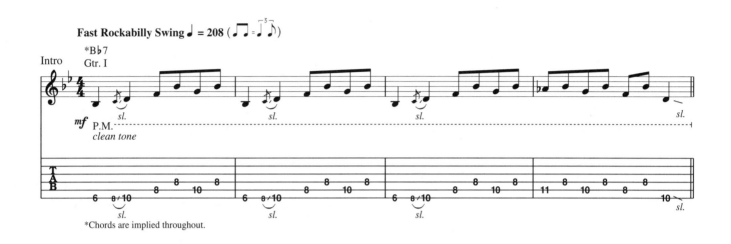

*Chords are implied throughout.

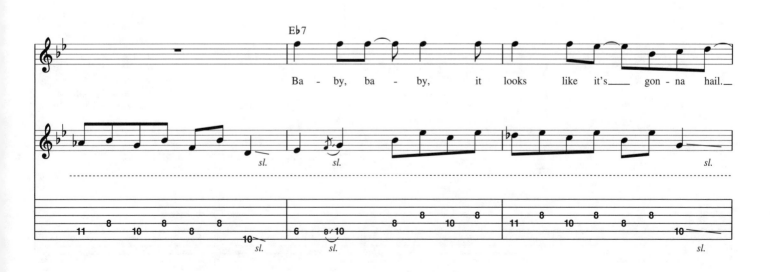

*Play w/slight variations ad lib on repeat.

*Depress bar before striking chord.

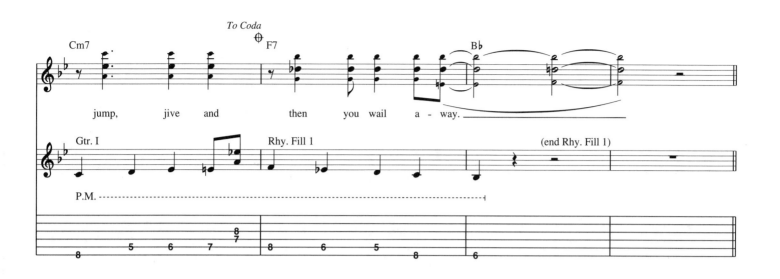

jump, jive and then you wail a-way.

Sax solo
w/Rhy. Fig. 1

2nd Verse
w/Rhy. Fig. 1 (1st 10 bars only)

Pa - pa's in the ice - box

look - in' for a ___ can of ale. ___ Pa - pa's in the ice - box

look - in' for a ___ can of ale. ___ Ma - ma's in the back - yard

D.S. al Coda

Gtrs.
I & II

learn - in' how to jive ___ and wail. ___ Woh, ___ you got - ta

then you wail a - way.

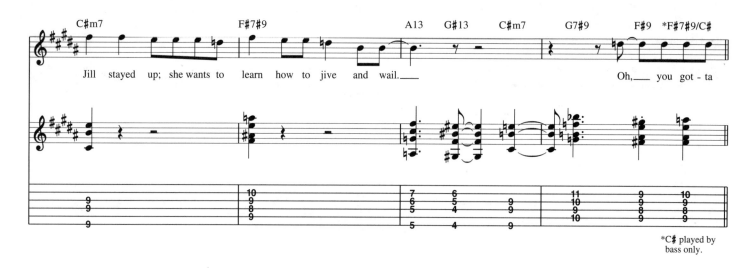

Jill stayed up; she wants to learn how to jive and wail.___ Oh,___ you got-ta

*C♯ played by
bass only.

Chorus
Tacet

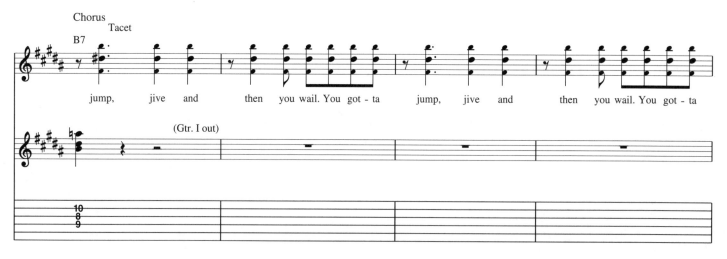

jump, jive and then you wail. You got-ta jump, jive and then you wail. You got-ta

(Gtr. I out)

jump, jive and then you wail. You got-ta jump, jive and then you wail. You got-ta

jump, jive and then you wail a - way.___ You got-ta

Chorus/Outro
w/Rhy. Fig. 2

jump, jive and then you wail. You got-ta jump, jive and then you wail. You got-ta

jump, jive and then you wail. You got-ta jump, jive and then you wail. You got-ta

More Than Words

Words and Music by Nuno Bettencourt and Gary Cherone

Tune down 1/2 step:
(low to high) E♭–A♭–D♭–G♭–B♭–E♭

* Hit muted strings w/ R.H. throughout.

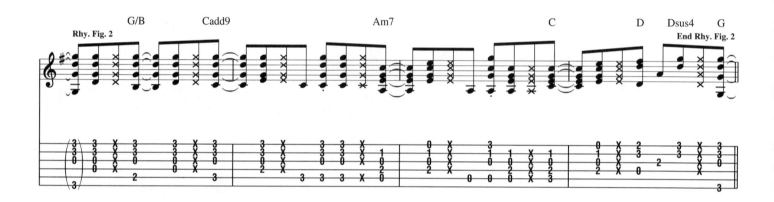

Verse

1. Say-ing "I ___ love ___ you" is not the words ___ I want ___ to hear ___ from you. ___

___ It's not that I ___ want ___ you not to say, ___ but if ___

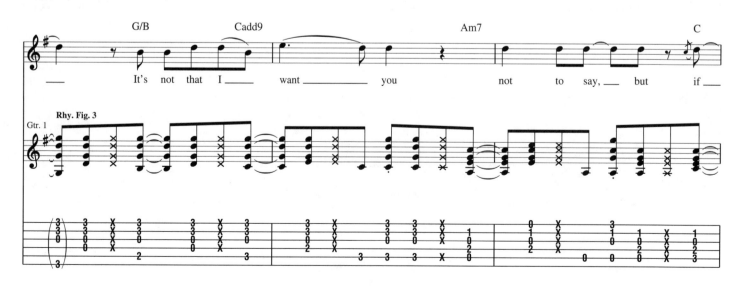

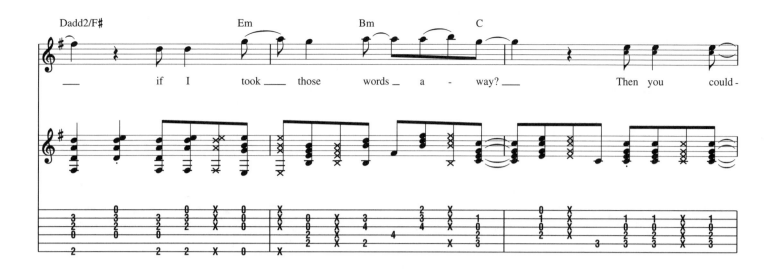

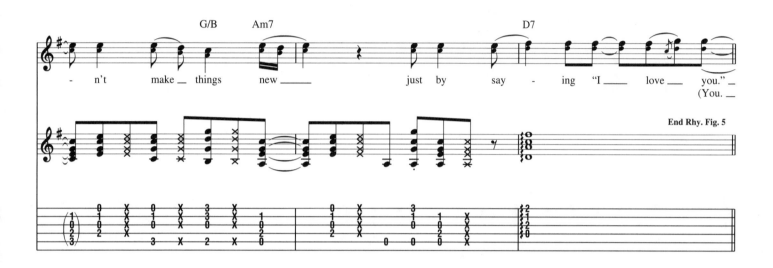

Interlude

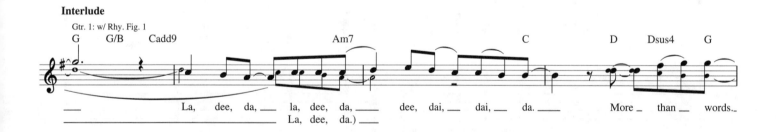

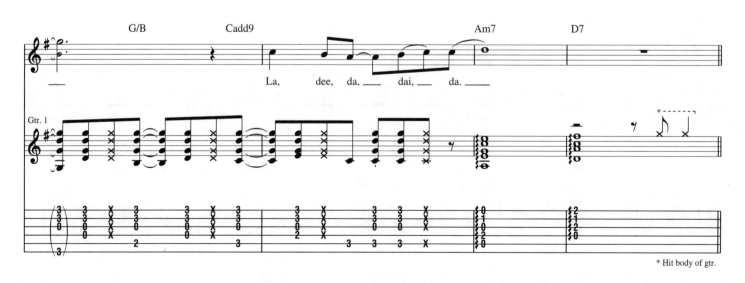

* Hit body of gtr.

Verse

Gtr. 1: w/ Rhy. Fig. 1

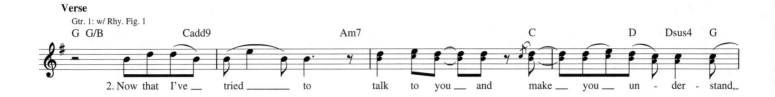

2. Now that I've tried to talk to you and make you un - der - stand,

Gtr. 1: w/ Rhy. Fig. 3

all you have to do is close your eyes and just

reach out your hands and touch me.

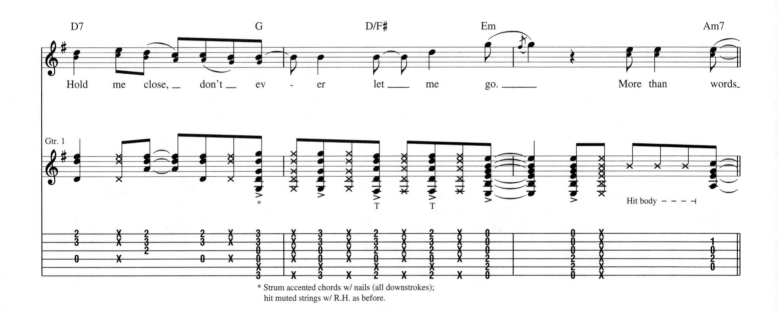

Hold me close, don't ev - er let me go. More than words.

Gtr. 1

* Strum accented chords w/ nails (all downstrokes);
hit muted strings w/ R.H. as before.

Chorus

Gtr. 1: w/ Rhy. Fig. 4

is all I ev - er need - ed you to show.

Then you would - n't have to say that you love me, 'cause

156

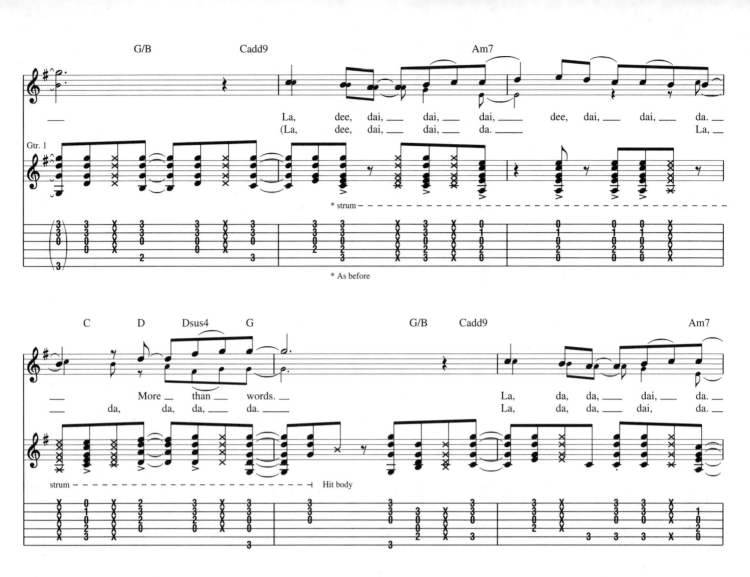

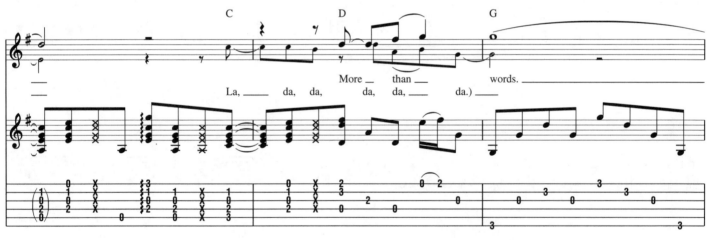

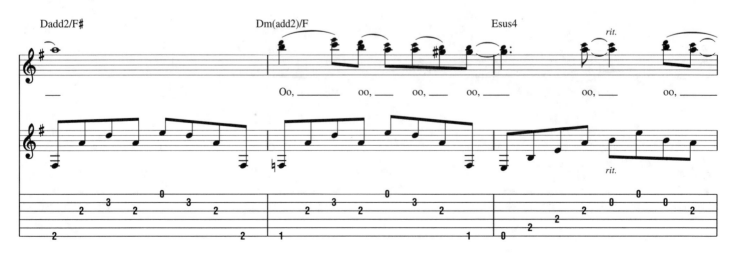

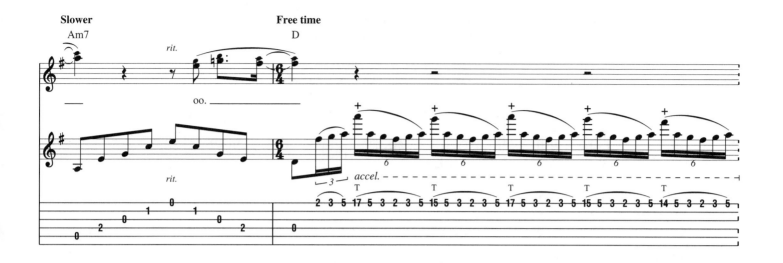

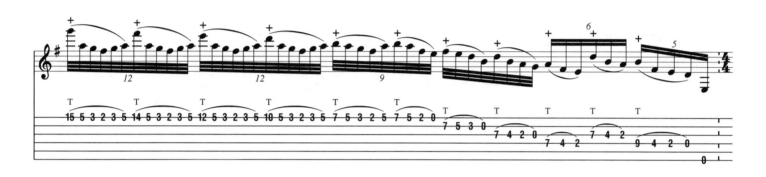

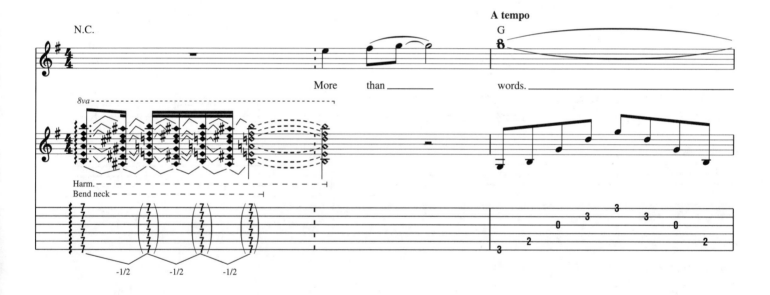

Santa Monica

Words by Art Alexakis

Music by Art Alexakis and Everclear

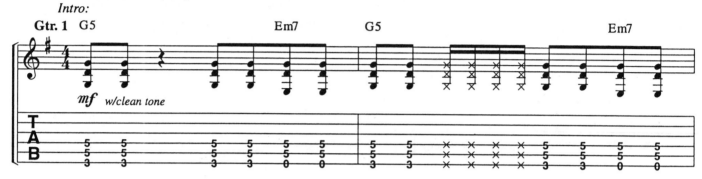

Moderate rock ♩ = 100

Intro:

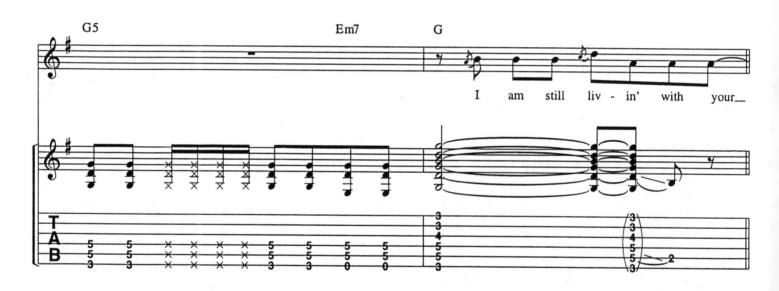

I am still liv-in' with your__

Verse 1:

— ghost,__ lone-ly and dream-ing of__ the__ West__

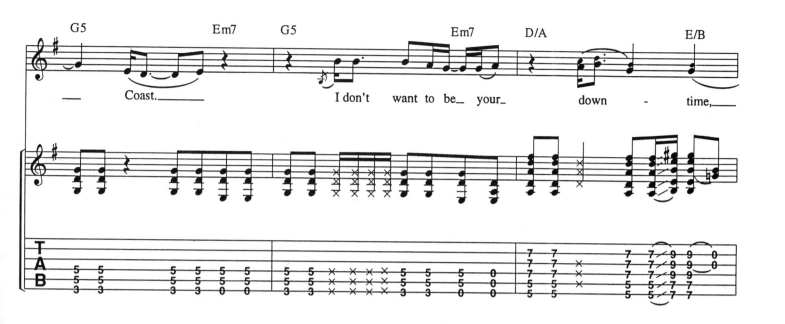

Coast._____ I don't want to be_ your_ down - time,_____

w/Rhy. Fill 1 *(Gtr. 2)*

_____ I don't want to be_ your stu - pid game.._ With my big black boots_ and an old suit -

Cont. in slashes

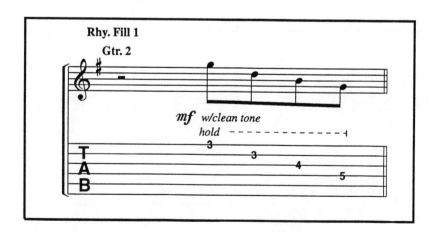

Rhy. Fill 1

Gtr. 2

mf *w/clean tone*

hold - - - - - - - - - - - - -

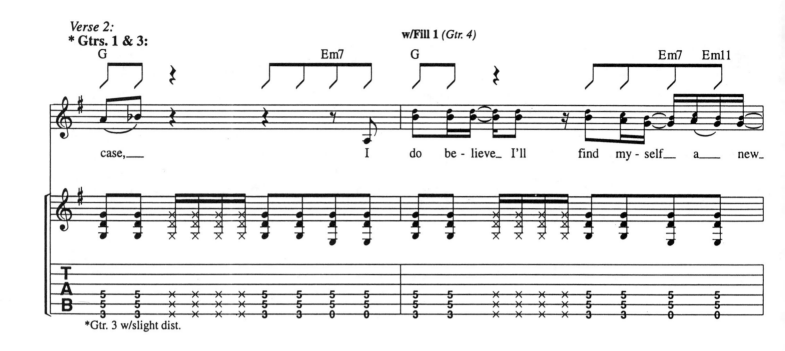

*Gtr. 3 w/slight dist.

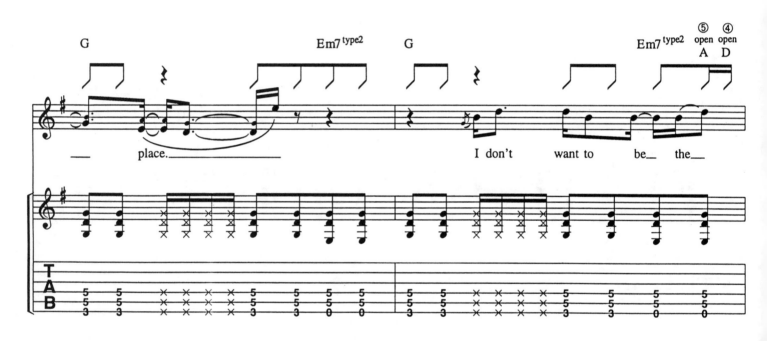

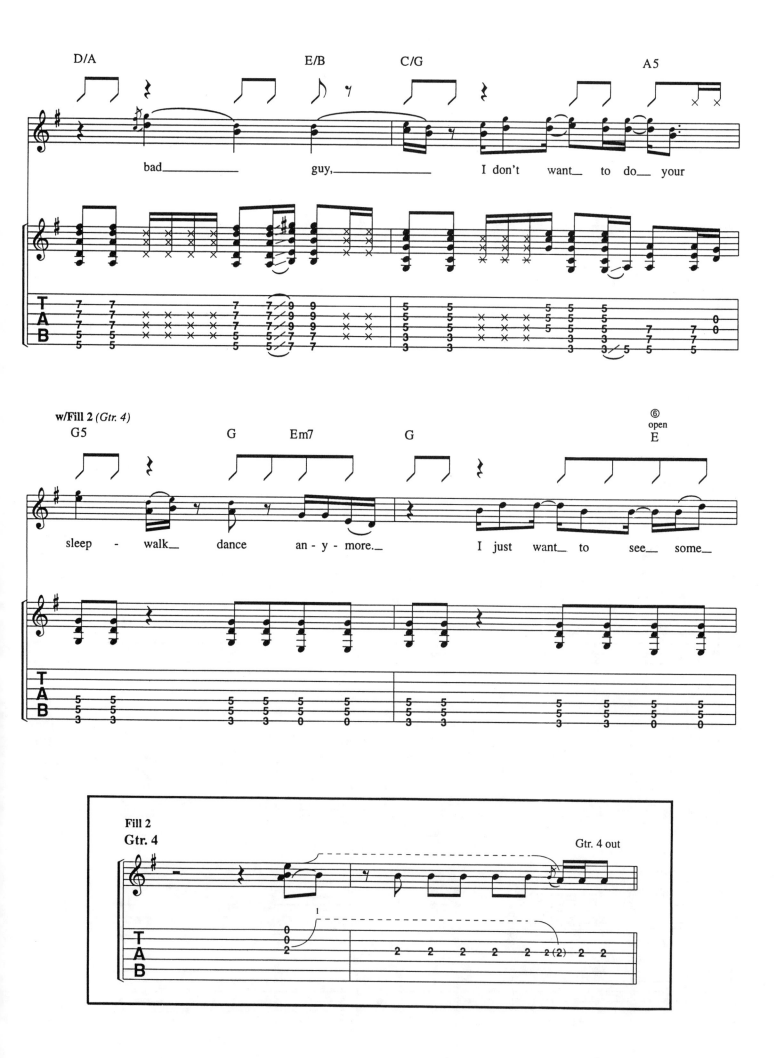

164

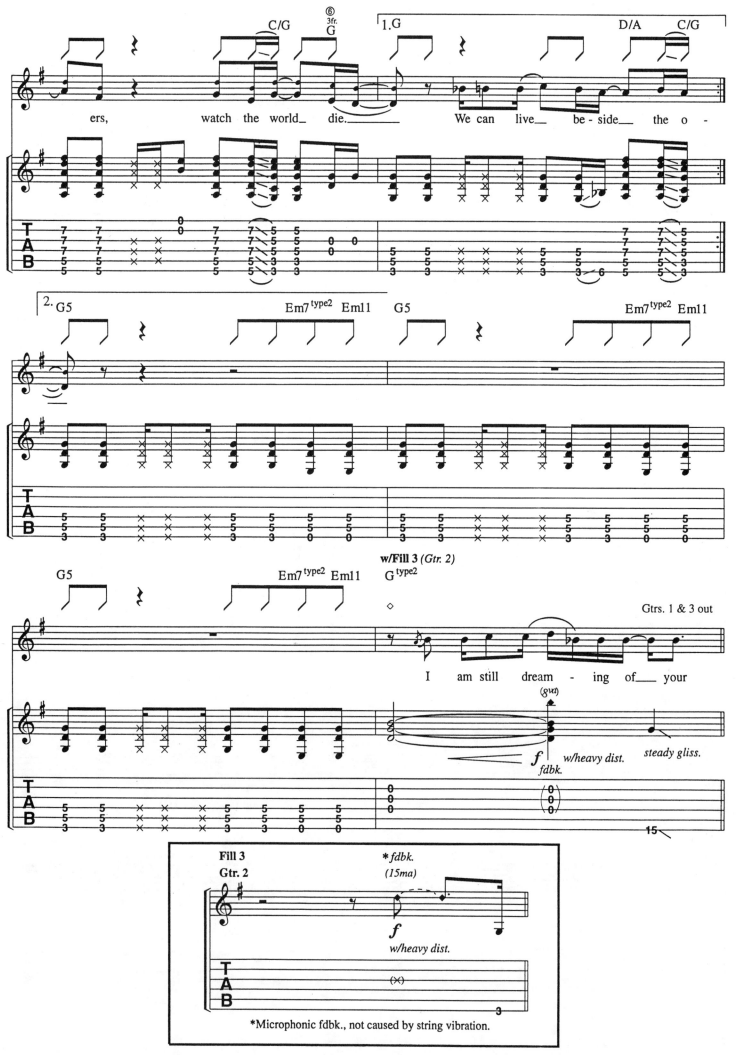

*Microphonic fdbk., not caused by string vibration.

Verse 3:

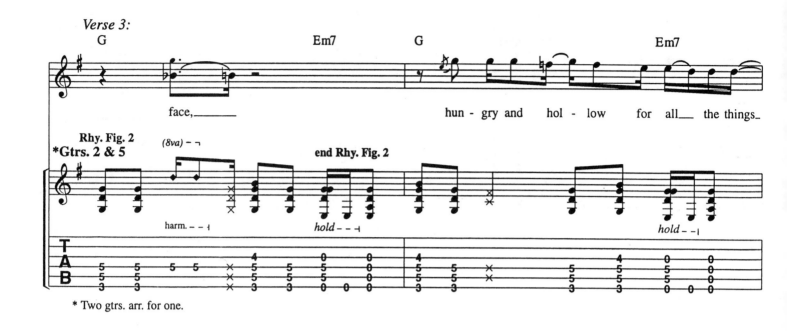

face,_____ hun - gry and hol - low for all___ the things___

* Two gtrs. arr. for one.

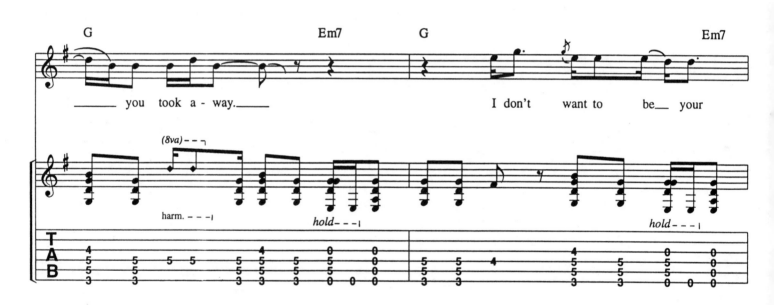

_____ you took a - way._____ I don't want to be___ your

good_____ time,_____ I don't want___ to be___ your

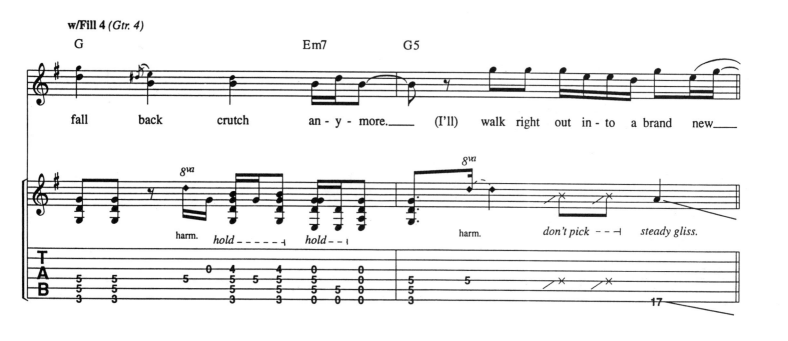

Verse 4:

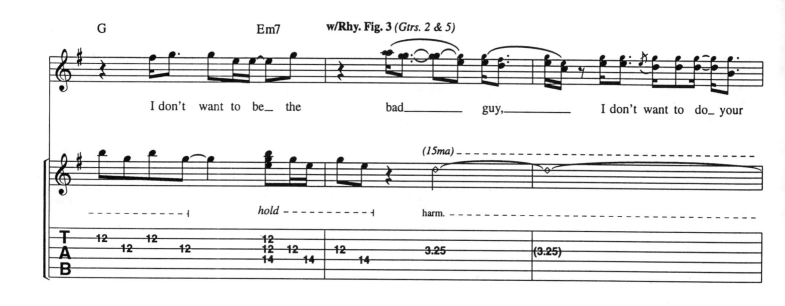

I don't want to be_ the bad_____ guy,_____ I don't want to do_ your

sleep - walk_ dance an- y- more.__ I just want. to feel_ some___ sun - shine,_____

— I just want_ to find_ some place to be a - lone._____

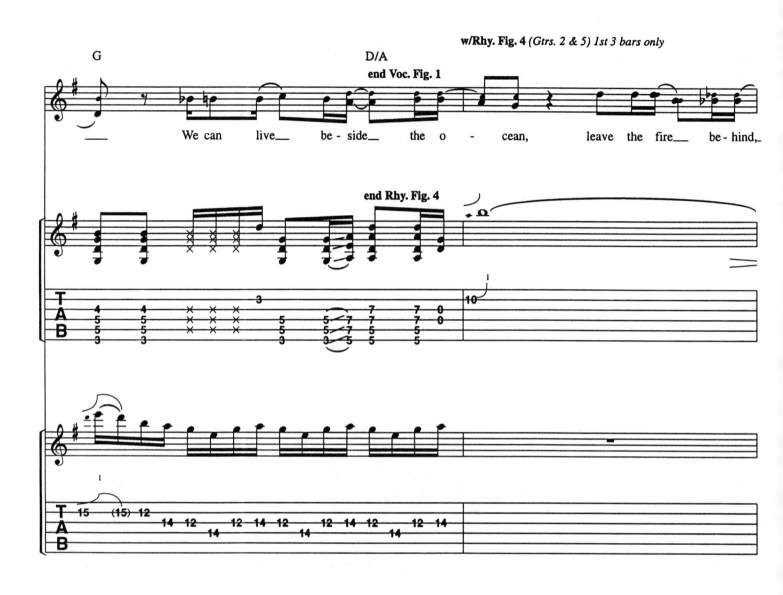

We can live___ be - side___ the o - cean, leave the fire___ be - hind,___

swim out past___ the break - ers, watch the world___ die.___

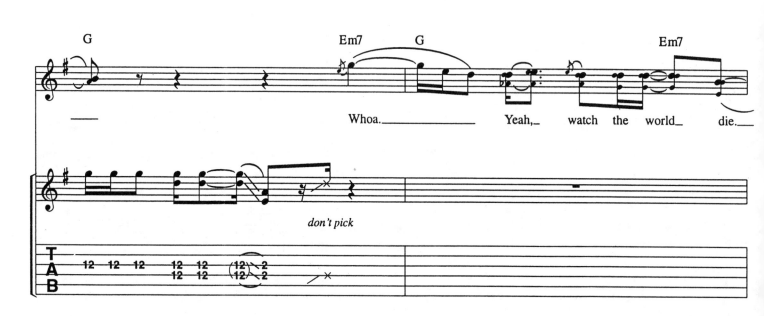

Semi-Charmed Life

Words and Music by Stephan Jenkins

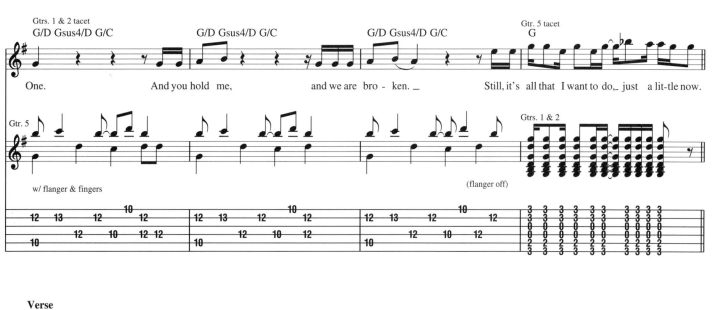

Verse

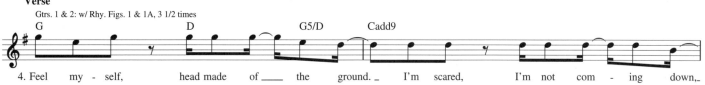

Chorus

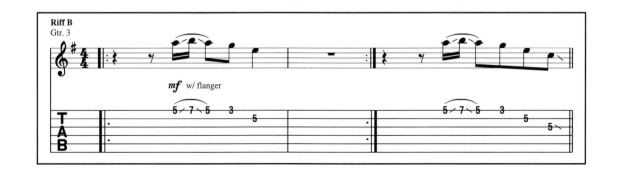

Silent Lucidity

Words and Music by Chris DeGarmo

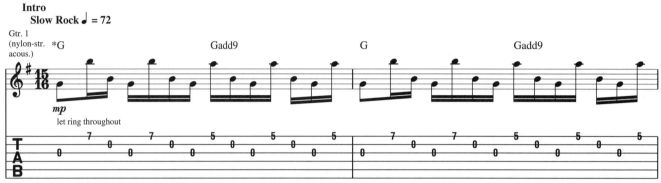

* Chord symbols reflect implied tonality.

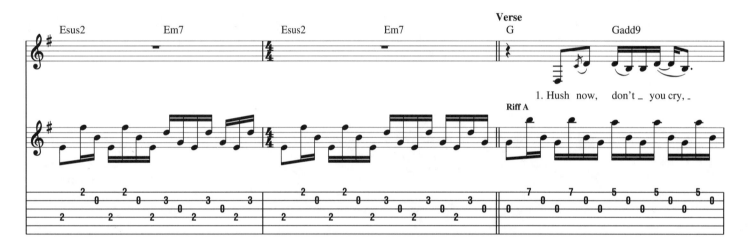

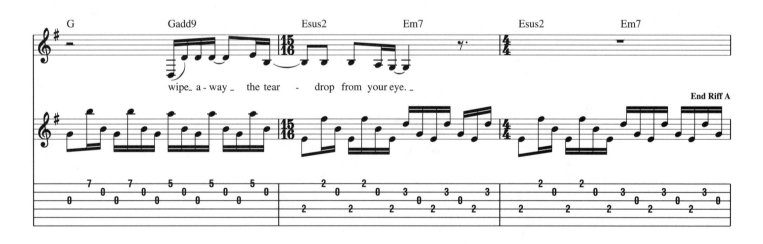

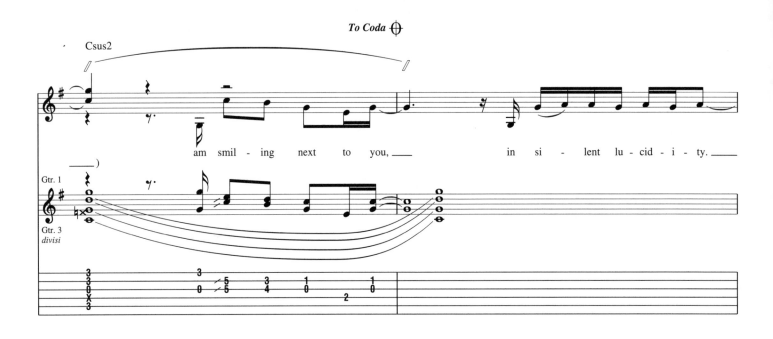

am smil - ing next to you, ____ in si - lent lu - cid - i - ty. ____

Guitar Solo

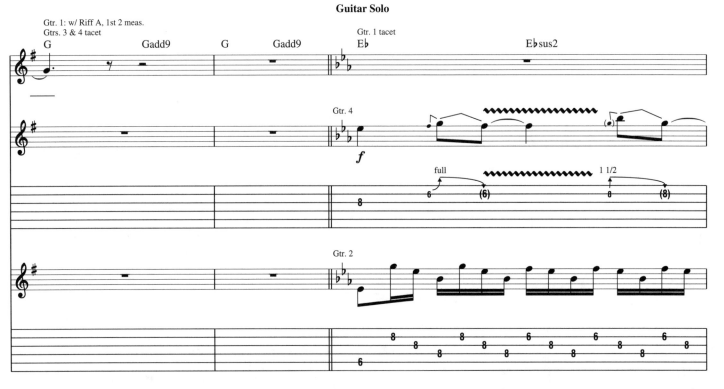

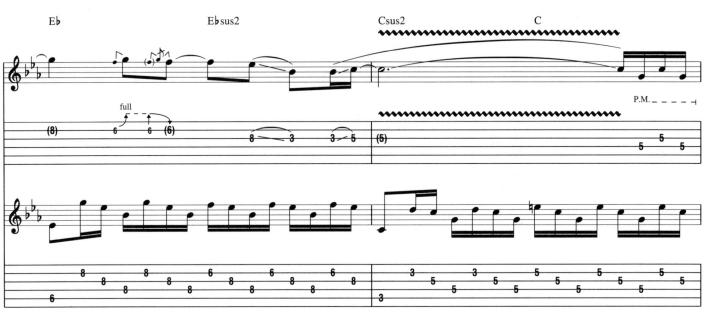

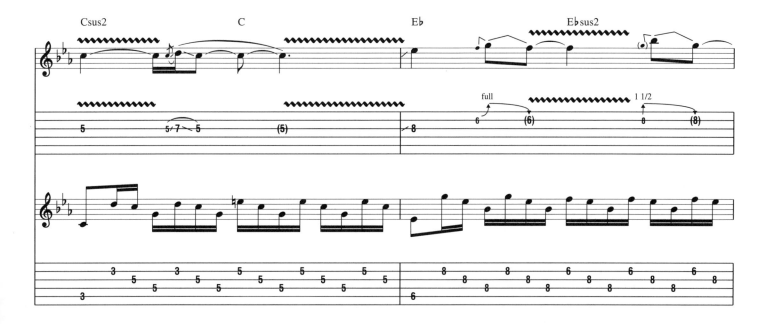

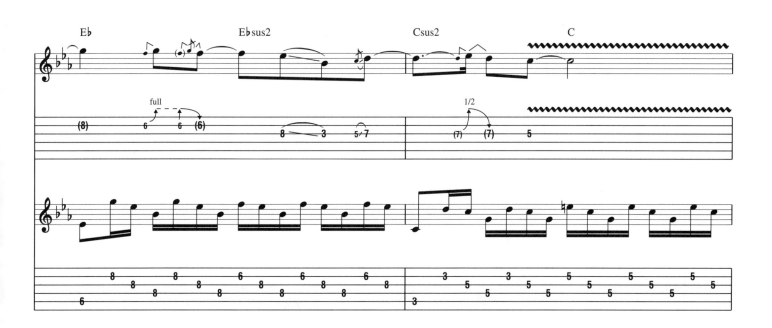

Spoken: *Visualize your dream, record it in the present*

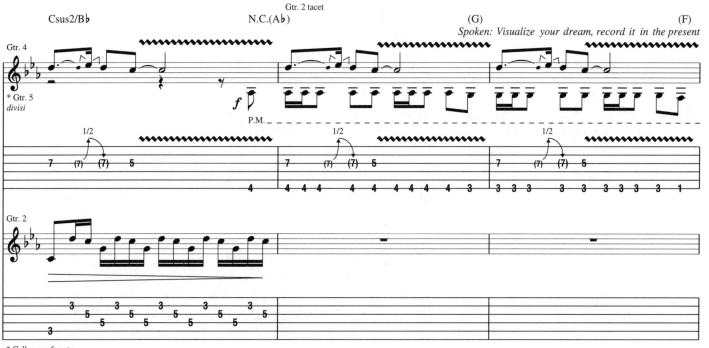

* Cellos arr. for gtr.

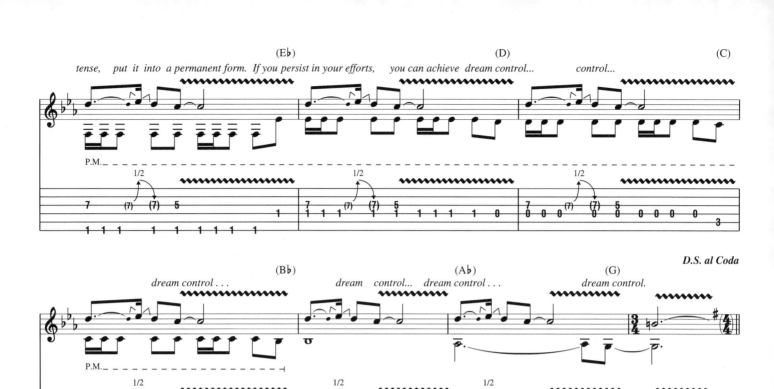

tense, put it into a permanent form. If you persist in your efforts, you can achieve dream control... control...

(E♭)   *(D)*   *(C)*

D.S. al Coda

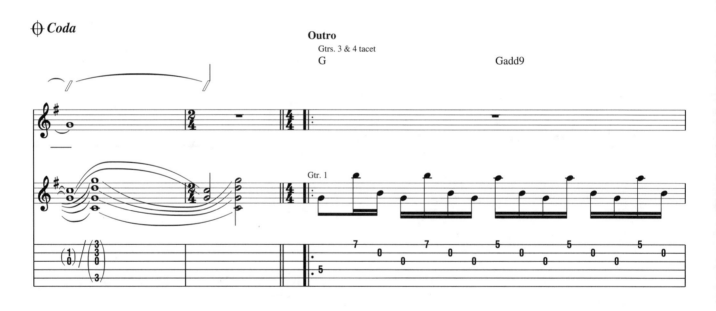

dream control . . .   *(B♭)*   *dream control... dream control . . .*   *(A♭)*   *dream control.*   *(G)*

⊕ *Coda*

Outro

Gtrs. 3 & 4 tacet

G   Gadd9

Gtr. 1

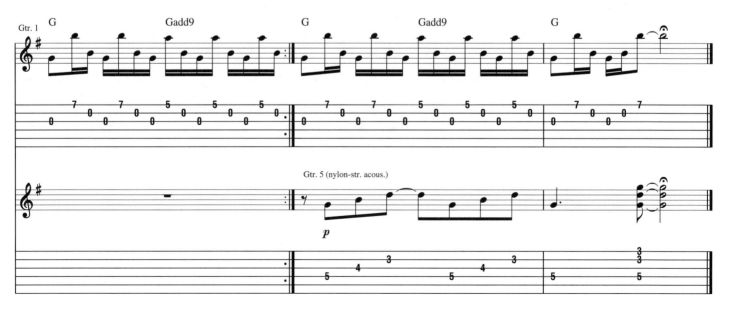

Gtr. 1   G   Gadd9   G   Gadd9   G

Gtr. 5 (nylon-str. acous.)

p

Smells Like Teen Spirit

Words and Music by Kurt Cobain, Chris Novoselic and David Grohl

Guitar Solo

Smooth

Words by Rob Thomas
Music by Rob Thomas and Itaal Shur

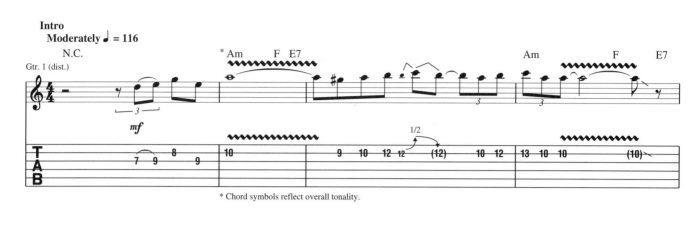

* Chord symbols reflect overall tonality.

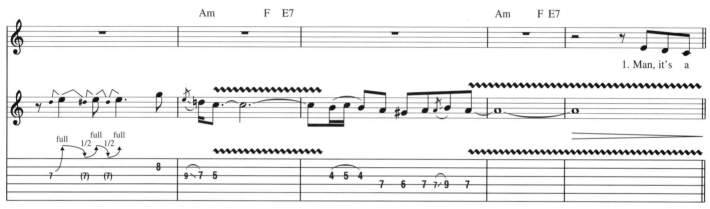

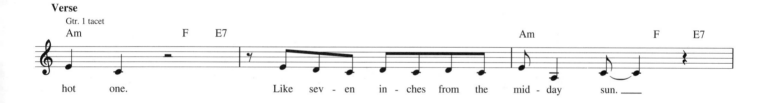

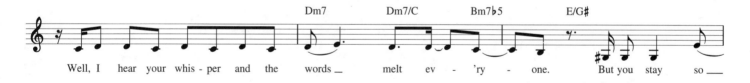

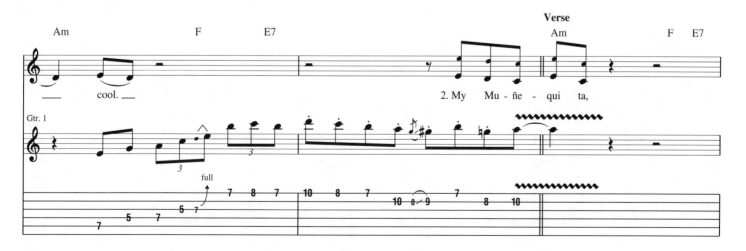

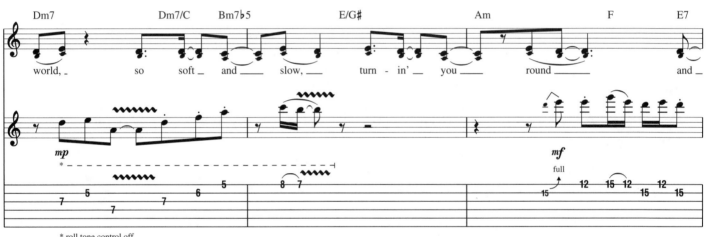

* roll tone control off.

Tears in Heaven

featured in the Motion Picture RUSH

Words and Music by Eric Clapton and Will Jennings

have ya beg - gin' please, beg-gin' please.

Interlude

Chorus

- yond the door there's peace, I'm sure,

if I saw you in hea - ven?

Coda

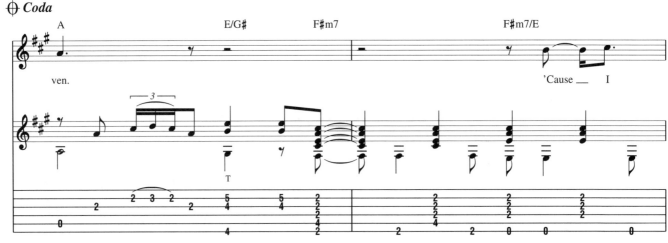

ven.   'Cause ___ I

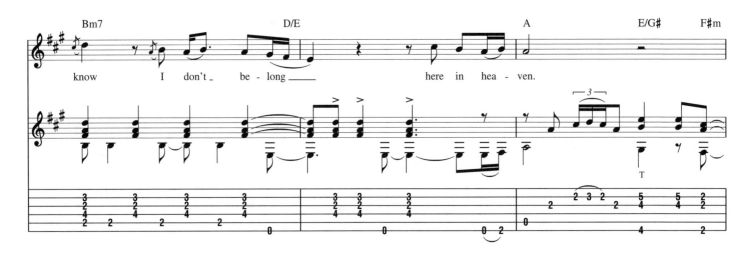

know   I don't _ be - long ___   here in hea - ven.

Freely

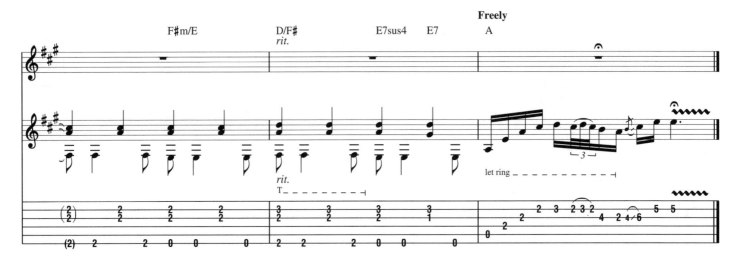

Two Princes

Words and Music by Spin Doctors

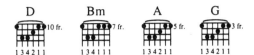

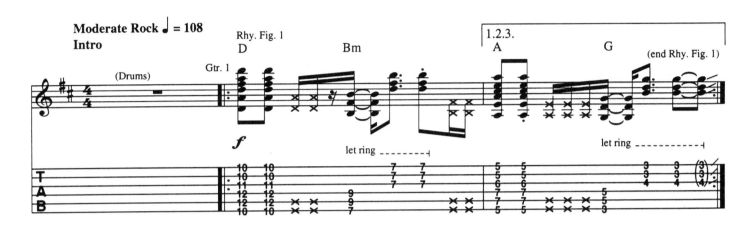

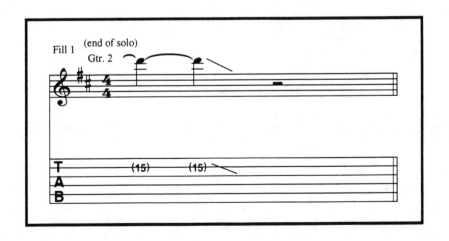

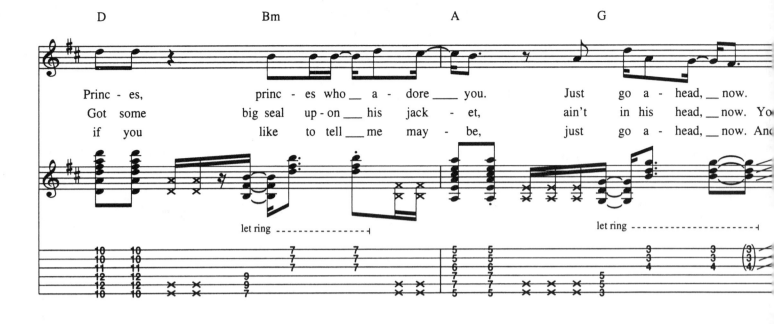

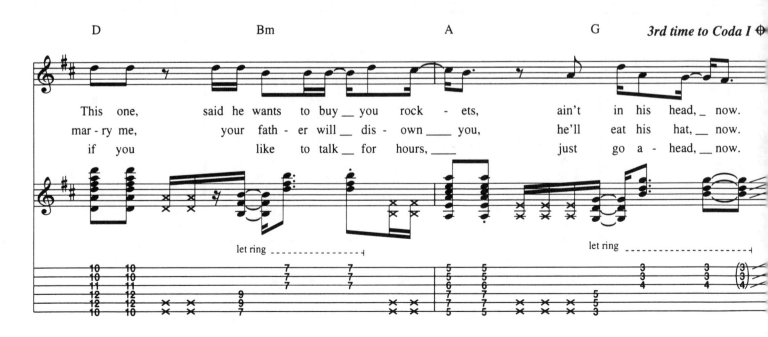

D. S. al Coda I 𝄋   Coda I   **Guitar Solo**

I know what a prince and lov-er ought to be. __ Said...

D   Bm7   A   G   D   Bm7

if you   like to tell __ me may - be,   just go a - head, _ now. And if you   like to buy _ me flow

A   G   D   Bm7   A   G

ers,   just go a-head, __ now. And if you   like to talk __ for hours, ___   just go a-head, __now.

D   Bm   A   G
w/Rhy. Fig. 1 (4 times)

If   you want to call me ___ ba - by,   just go a - head, __ now.

D   Bm   A   G

And if   you'd like to tell ___ me ___ may - be,   just go a - head, ___ now.

D   Bm   A   G   D   Bm

If   you want to buy me flow - ers,   just   go a - head, __ now.   And if you like to talk for hours,

A   G   D   Bm7   A   G
w/Rhy. Fig. 2 (2 times)

___   just go a - head, _ now.   Oh, _____ ba - by.   Oh,
                                 (Just go a - head, _ now.)

D   Bm7   A   G   D   Bm7

_____ oh, _____ just, just   go a - head, __ now.   Oh, _____ your __ maj
                            (Just   go a - head, ___now.)

A   G   D   Bm7

es - ty, _____   come on __ for - get ___ the king ___ and
      (Just   go a - head, __ now.)

A   G   D   Bm7   A   G   *Repeat and fade*
                                 w/Rhy. Fig. 1
                                 (cont. Lead voc. ad lib)

mar - ry me. _____   (Just go a - head, __ now.)
   (Just   go a - head, _ now.)

Under the Bridge

Words and Music by Anthony Kiedis, Flea, John Frusciante and Chad Smith

Wonderwall

Words and Music by Noel Gallagher

* Symbols in parentheses represent chord names respective to capoed guitars.
  Symbols above reflect actual sounding chords.

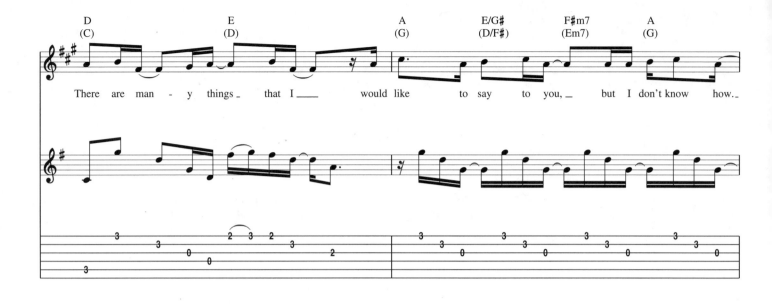

There are man - y things __ that I ___ would like to say to you, __ but I don't know how..

Be-cause
I said

(cont. in slash)

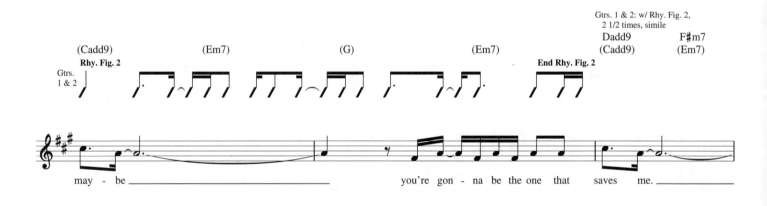

may - be _____ you're gon - na be the one that saves me. _____

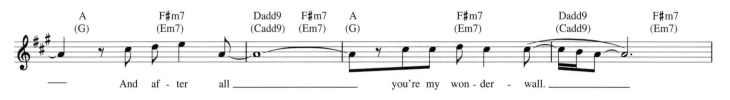

And af - ter all _____ you're my won - der - wall. _____

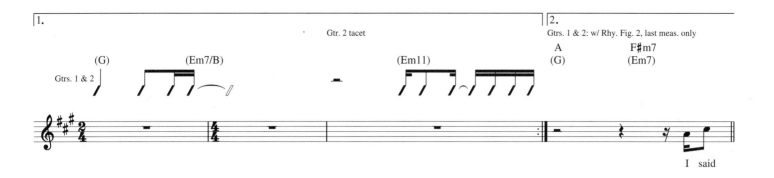

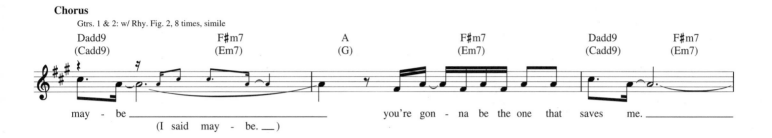

Chorus

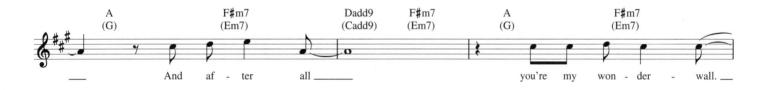

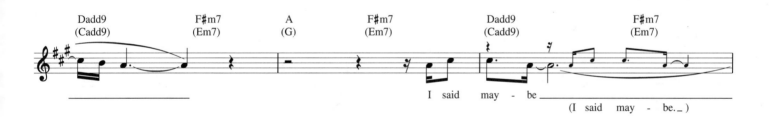

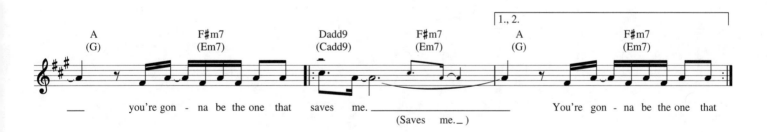

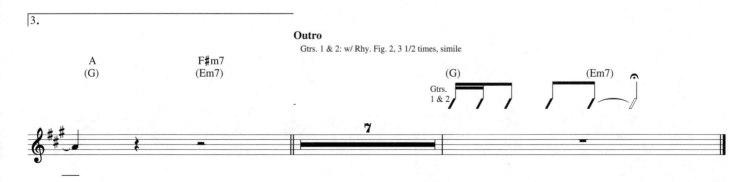

Guitar Notation Legend

Guitar Music can be notated three different ways: on a *musical staff*, in *tablature*, and in *rhythm slashes*.

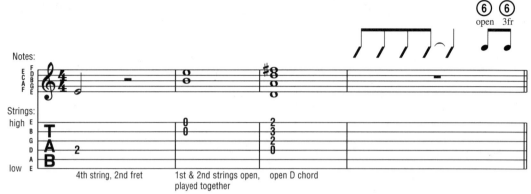

RHYTHM SLASHES are written above the staff. Strum chords in the rhythm indicated. Use the chord diagrams found at the top of the first page of the transcription for the appropriate chord voicings. Round noteheads indicate single notes.

THE MUSICAL STAFF shows pitches and rhythms and is divided by bar lines into measures. Pitches are named after the first seven letters of the alphabet.

TABLATURE graphically represents the guitar fingerboard. Each horizontal line represents a string, and each number represents a fret.

HALF-STEP BEND: Strike the note and bend up 1/2 step.

BEND AND RELEASE: Strike the note and bend up as indicated, then release back to the original note. Only the first note is struck.

HAMMER-ON: Strike the first (lower) note with one finger, then sound the higher note (on the same string) with another finger by fretting it without picking.

TRILL: Very rapidly alternate between the notes indicated by continuously hammering on and pulling off.

PICK SCRAPE: The edge of the pick is rubbed down (or up) the string, producing a scratchy sound.

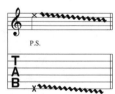

TREMOLO PICKING: The note is picked as rapidly and continuously as possible.

WHOLE-STEP BEND: Strike the note and bend up one step.

PRE-BEND: Bend the note as indicated, then strike it.

PULL-OFF: Place both fingers on the notes to be sounded. Strike the first note and without picking, pull the finger off to sound the second (lower) note.

TAPPING: Hammer ("tap") the fret indicated with the pick-hand index or middle finger and pull off to the note fretted by the fret hand.

MUFFLED STRINGS: A percussive sound is produced by laying the fret hand across the string(s) without depressing, and striking them with the pick hand.

VIBRATO BAR DIVE AND RETURN: The pitch of the note or chord is dropped a specified number of steps (in rhythm) then returned to the original pitch.

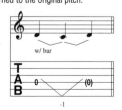

GRACE NOTE BEND: Strike the note and immediately bend up as indicated.

VIBRATO: The string is vibrated by rapidly bending and releasing the note with the fretting hand.

LEGATO SLIDE: Strike the first note and then slide the same fret-hand finger up or down to the second note. The second note is not struck.

NATURAL HARMONIC: Strike the note while the fret-hand lightly touches the string directly over the fret indicated.

PALM MUTING: The note is partially muted by the pick hand lightly touching the string(s) just before the bridge.

VIBRATO BAR SCOOP: Depress the bar just before striking the note, then quickly release the bar.

SLIGHT (MICROTONE) BEND: Strike the note and bend up 1/4 step.

WIDE VIBRATO: The pitch is varied to a greater degree by vibrating with the fretting hand.

SHIFT SLIDE: Same as legato slide, except the second note is struck.

PINCH HARMONIC: The note is fretted normally and a harmonic is produced by adding the edge of the thumb or the tip of the index finger of the pick hand to the normal pick attack.

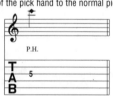

RAKE: Drag the pick across the strings indicated with a single motion.

VIBRATO BAR DIP: Strike the note and then immediately drop a specified number of steps, then release back to the original pitch.

THE DECADE SERIES

These collections, especially for guitarists, feature the top tunes that shaped a decade, transcribed note-for-note.

The 1950s

35 pivotal songs from the early rock years: All Shook Up • Be-Bop-a-Lula • Bo Diddley • Boppin' the Blues • Cannonball • Donna • Foggy Mountain Breakdown • Get Rhythm • Guitar Boogie Shuffle • Heartbreak Hotel • Hound Dog • I'm Lookin' for Someone to Love • I'm Movin' On • I'm Your Hoochie Coochie Man • Lonesome Town • Matchbox • Moonlight in Vermont • My Babe • Poor Little Fool • Put Your Cat Clothes On • Race With the Devil • Rebel 'Rouser • Reconsider Baby • Rock Around the Clock • Rocket '88 • Rockin' Robin • Sleepwalk • Slippin' and Slidin' • Susie-Q • Sweet Little Angel • Tequila • (They Call It) Stormy Monday (Stormy Monday Blues) • Wake Up Little Susie • The World Is Waiting for the Sunrise • Yankee Doodle Dixie

_____00690543 **Guitar Recorded Versions** $14.95

The 1960s

30 songs that defined the '60s: Badge • Blackbird • Fun, Fun, Fun • Gloria • Good Lovin' • Green Onions • Happy Together • Hello Mary Lou • Hey Joe • Hush • I Can See for Miles • I Feel Fine • I Get Around • In the Midnight Hour • Jingo (Jin-Go-Lo-Ba) • Let's Live for Today • Louie, Louie • My Girl • Oh, Pretty Woman • On the Road Again • The Promised Land • Somebody to Love • Soul Man • Suite: Judy Blue Eyes • Susie-Q • Time Is on My Side • (So) Tired of Waiting for You • Train Kept A-Rollin' • Walk Don't Run • Wild Thing

_____00690542 **Guitar Recorded Versions** $14.95

The 1970s

30 top songs from the '70s: Barracuda • Best of My Love • Blue Collar Man (Long Nights) • Breakdown • Burning Love • Dust in the Wind • Evil Woman • Freeway Jam • Godzilla • Happy • Landslide • Lay Down Sally • Let It Be • Maggie May • No Woman No Cry • Oye Como Va • Paranoid • Rock and Roll Hoochie Koo • Show Me the Way • Smoke on the Water • So Into You • Space Oddity • Stayin' Alive • Teach Your Children • Time in a Bottle • Walk This Way • Wheel in the Sky • You Ain't Seen Nothin' Yet • You Really Got Me • You've Got a Friend

_____00690541 **Guitar Recorded Versions** $15.95

The 1980s

30 songs that best represent the decade: Caught Up in You • Down Boys • 867-5309/Jenny • Every Breath You Take • Eye of the Tiger • Fight for Your Right (To Party) • Heart and Soul • Hit Me With Your Best Shot • I Love Rock 'N Roll • In and Out of Love • La Bamba • Land of Confusion • Love Struck Baby • (Bang Your Head) Metal Health • Money for Nothing • Mony, Mony • Rag Doll • Refugee • R.O.C.K. in the U.S.A. (A Salute to '60s Rock) • Rock Me • Rock You Like a Hurricane • Running on Faith • Seventeen • Start Me Up • Summer of '69 • Sweet Child O' Mine • Wait • What I Like About You • Working for the Weekend • You May Be Right

_____00690540 **Guitar Recorded Versions** $15.95

The 1990s

30 essential '90s classics: All I Wanna Do • Are You Gonna Go My Way • Barely Breathing • Blue on Black • Boot Scootin' Boogie • Building a Mystery • Bulls on Parade • Come Out and Play • Cryin' • (Everything I Do) I Do It for You • Fields of Gold • Free As a Bird • Friends in Low Places • Give Me One Reason • Hold My Hand • I Can't Dance • I'm the Only One • The Impression That I Get • Iris • Jump, Jive an' Wail • More Than Words • Santa Monica • Semi-Charmed Life • Silent Lucidity • Smells Like Teen Spirit • Smooth • Tears in Heaven • Two Princes • Under the Bridge • Wonderwall

_____00690539 **Guitar Recorded Versions** $15.95

RECORDED VERSIONS
The Best Note-For-Note Transcriptions Available

ALL BOOKS INCLUDE TABLATURE

00690016 Will Ackerman Collection	$19.95
00690146 Aerosmith – Toys in the Attic	$19.95
00694865 Alice In Chains – Dirt	$19.95
00694932 Allman Brothers Band – Volume 1	$24.95
00694933 Allman Brothers Band – Volume 2	$24.95
00694934 Allman Brothers Band – Volume 3	$24.95
00694877 Chet Atkins – Guitars For All Seasons	$19.95
00690418 Best of Audio Adrenaline	$17.95
00694918 Randy Bachman Collection	$22.95
00690366 Bad Company Original Anthology - Bk 1	$19.95
00690367 Bad Company Original Anthology - Bk 2	$19.95
00694880 Beatles – Abbey Road	$19.95
00694863 Beatles – Sgt. Pepper's Lonely Hearts Club Band	$19.95
00690383 Beatles – Yellow Submarine	$19.95
00690174 Beck – Mellow Gold	$17.95
00690346 Beck – Mutations	$19.95
00690175 Beck – Odelay	$17.95
00694884 The Best of George Benson	$19.95
00692385 Chuck Berry	$19.95
00692200 Black Sabbath – We Sold Our Soul For Rock 'N' Roll	$19.95
00690115 Blind Melon – Soup	$19.95
00690305 Blink 182 – Dude Ranch	$19.95
00690028 Blue Oyster Cult – Cult Classics	$19.95
00690219 Blur	$19.95
00690168 Roy Buchanon Collection	$19.95
00690364 Cake – Songbook	$19.95
00690337 Jerry Cantrell – Boggy Depot	$19.95
00690293 Best of Steven Curtis Chapman	$19.95
00690043 Cheap Trick – Best Of	$19.95
00690171 Chicago – Definitive Guitar Collection	$22.95
00690415 Clapton Chronicles – Best of Eric Clapton	$17.95
00690393 Eric Clapton – Selections from Blues	$19.95
00660139 Eric Clapton – Journeyman	$19.95
00694869 Eric Clapton – Live Acoustic	$19.95
00694896 John Mayall/Eric Clapton – Bluesbreakers	$19.95
00690162 Best of the Clash	$19.95
00690166 Albert Collins – The Alligator Years	$16.95
00694940 Counting Crows – August & Everything After	$19.95
00690197 Counting Crows – Recovering the Satellites	$19.95
00694840 Cream – Disraeli Gears	$19.95
00690401 Creed – Human Clay	$19.95
00690352 Creed – My Own Prison	$19.95
00690184 dc Talk – Jesus Freak	$19.95
00690333 dc Talk – Supernatural	$19.95
00660186 Alex De Grassi Guitar Collection	$19.95
00690289 Best of Deep Purple	$17.95
00694831 Derek And The Dominos – Layla & Other Assorted Love Songs	$19.95
00690322 Ani Di Franco – Little Plastic Castle	$19.95
00690187 Dire Straits – Brothers In Arms	$19.95
00690191 Dire Straits – Money For Nothing	$24.95
00695382 The Very Best of Dire Straits – Sultans of Swing	$19.95
00660178 Willie Dixon – Master Blues Composer	$24.95
00690250 Best of Duane Eddy	$16.95
00690349 Eve 6	$19.95
00313164 Eve 6 – Horrorscope	$19.95
00690323 Fastball – All the Pain Money Can Buy	$19.95
00690089 Foo Fighters	$19.95
00690235 Foo Fighters – The Colour and the Shape	$19.95
00690394 Foo Fighters – There Is Nothing Left to Lose	$19.95
00690222 G3 Live – Satriani, Vai, Johnson	$22.95
00694807 Danny Gatton – 88 Elmira St	$19.95
00690438 Genesis Guitar Anthology	$19.95

00690127 Goo Goo Dolls – A Boy Named Goo	$19.95
00690338 Goo Goo Dolls – Dizzy Up the Girl	$19.95
00690117 John Gorka Collection	$19.95
00690114 Buddy Guy Collection Vol. A-J	$22.95
00690193 Buddy Guy Collection Vol. L-Y	$22.95
00694798 George Harrison Anthology	$19.95
00690068 Return Of The Hellecasters	$19.95
00692930 Jimi Hendrix – Are You Experienced?	$24.95
00692931 Jimi Hendrix – Axis: Bold As Love	$22.95
00692932 Jimi Hendrix – Electric Ladyland	$24.95
00690218 Jimi Hendrix – First Rays of the New Rising Sun	$27.95
00690038 Gary Hoey – Best Of	$19.95
00660029 Buddy Holly	$19.95
00660169 John Lee Hooker – A Blues Legend	$19.95
00690054 Hootie & The Blowfish – Cracked Rear View	$19.95
00694905 Howlin' Wolf	$19.95
00690136 Indigo Girls – 1200 Curfews	$22.95
00694938 Elmore James – Master Electric Slide Guitar	$19.95
00690167 Skip James Blues Guitar Collection	$16.95
00694833 Billy Joel For Guitar	$19.95
00694912 Eric Johnson – Ah Via Musicom	$19.95
00690169 Eric Johnson – Venus Isle	$22.95
00694799 Robert Johnson – At The Crossroads	$19.95
00693185 Judas Priest – Vintage Hits	$19.95
00690277 Best of Kansas	$19.95
00690073 B. B. King – 1950-1957	$24.95
00690098 B. B. King – 1958-1967	$24.95
00690444 B.B. King and Eric Clapton – Riding with the King	$19.95
00690134 Freddie King Collection	$17.95
00690157 Kiss – Alive	$19.95
00690163 Mark Knopfler/Chet Atkins – Neck and Neck	$19.95
00690296 Patty Larkin Songbook	$17.95
00690018 Living Colour – Best Of	$19.95
00694845 Yngwie Malmsteen – Fire And Ice	$19.95
00694956 Bob Marley – Legend	$19.95
00690283 Best of Sarah McLachlan	$19.95
00690382 Sarah McLachlan – Mirrorball	$19.95
00690354 Sarah McLachlan – Surfacing	$19.95
00690442 Matchbox 20 – Mad Season	$19.95
00690239 Matchbox 20 – Yourself or Someone Like You	$19.95
00690244 Megadeath – Cryptic Writings	$19.95
00690236 Mighty Mighty Bosstones – Let's Face It	$19.95
00690040 Steve Miller Band Greatest Hits	$19.95
00694802 Gary Moore – Still Got The Blues	$19.95
00694958 Mountain, Best Of	$19.95
00690448 MxPx – The Ever Passing Moment	$19.95
00694913 Nirvana – In Utero	$19.95
00694883 Nirvana – Nevermind	$19.95
00690026 Nirvana – Acoustic In New York	$19.95
00690121 Oasis – (What's The Story) Morning Glory	$19.95
00690204 Offspring, The – Ixnay on the Hombre	$17.95
00690203 Offspring, The – Smash	$17.95
00694830 Ozzy Osbourne – No More Tears	$19.95
00694855 Pearl Jam – Ten	$19.95
00690053 Liz Phair – Whip Smart	$19.95
00690176 Phish – Billy Breathes	$22.95
00690424 Phish – Farmhouse	$19.95
00690331 Phish – The Story of Ghost	$19.95
00690428 Pink Floyd – Dark Side of the Moon	$19.95
00693800 Pink Floyd – Early Classics	$19.95
00690456 P.O.D. – The Fundamental Elements of Southtown	$19.95
00694967 Police – Message In A Box Boxed Set	$70.00
00694974 Queen – A Night At The Opera	$19.95

00690395 Rage Against The Machine – The Battle of Los Angeles	$19.95
00690145 Rage Against The Machine – Evil Empire	$19.95
00690179 Rancid – And Out Come the Wolves	$22.95
00690055 Red Hot Chili Peppers – Bloodsugarsexmagik	$19.95
00690379 Red Hot Chili Peppers – Californication	$19.95
00690090 Red Hot Chili Peppers – One Hot Minute	$22.95
00694937 Jimmy Reed – Master Bluesman	$19.95
00694899 R.E.M. – Automatic For The People	$19.95
00690260 Jimmie Rodgers Guitar Collection	$19.95
00690014 Rolling Stones – Exile On Main Street	$24.95
00690186 Rolling Stones – Rock & Roll Circus	$19.95
00690135 Otis Rush Collection	$19.95
00690031 Santana's Greatest Hits	$19.95
00690150 Son Seals – Bad Axe Blues	$17.95
00690128 Seven Mary Three – American Standards	$19.95
00120105 Kenny Wayne Shepherd – Ledbetter Heights	$19.95
00120123 Kenny Wayne Shepherd – Trouble Is	$19.95
00690196 Silverchair – Freak Show	$19.95
00690130 Silverchair – Frogstomp	$19.95
00690041 Smithereens – Best Of	$19.95
00690385 Sonicflood	$19.95
00694885 Spin Doctors – Pocket Full Of Kryptonite	$19.95
00694921 Steppenwolf, The Best Of	$22.95
00694957 Rod Stewart – Acoustic Live	$22.95
00690021 Sting – Fields Of Gold	$19.95
00690242 Suede – Coming Up	$19.95
00694824 Best of James Taylor	$16.95
00690238 Third Eye Blind	$19.95
00690403 Third Eye Blind – Blue	$19.95
00690267 311	$19.95
00690030 Toad The Wet Sprocket	$19.95
00690228 Tonic – Lemon Parade	$19.95
00690295 Tool – Aenima	$19.95
00690039 Steve Vai – Alien Love Secrets	$24.95
00690172 Steve Vai – Fire Garden	$24.95
00690023 Jimmie Vaughan – Strange Pleasures	$19.95
00690370 Stevie Ray Vaughan and Double Trouble – The Real Deal: Greatest Hits Volume 2	$22.95
00690455 Stevie Ray Vaughan – Blues at Sunrise	$19.95
00660136 Stevie Ray Vaughan – In Step	$19.95
00690417 Stevie Ray Vaughan – Live at Carnegie Hall	$19.95
00694835 Stevie Ray Vaughan – The Sky Is Crying	$19.95
00694776 Vaughan Brothers – Family Style	$19.95
00120026 Joe Walsh – Look What I Did...	$24.95
00694789 Muddy Waters – Deep Blues	$24.95
00690071 Weezer	$19.95
00690286 Weezer – Pinkerton	$19.95
00690447 Who, The – Best of	$24.95
00694970 Who, The – Definitive Collection A-E	$24.95
00694971 Who, The – Definitive Collection F-Li	$24.95
00694972 Who, The – Definitive Collection Lo-R	$24.95
00694973 Who, The – Definitive Collection S-Y	$24.95
00690319 Stevie Wonder Hits	$17.95

Prices and availability subject to change without notice.
Some products may not be available outside the U.S.A.

FOR A COMPLETE LIST OF GUITAR RECORDED VERSIONS TITLES, SEE YOUR LOCAL MUSIC DEALER, OR WRITE TO:

HAL•LEONARD® CORPORATION
7777 W. BLUEMOUND RD. P.O. BOX 13819 MILWAUKEE, WI 53213

Visit Hal Leonard online at www.halleonard.com   0401